Written Exercises
for the **Police Recruit**
Assessment Process

Written Exercises
for the **Police Recruit**
Assessment Process

Richard Malthouse
Jodi Roffey-Barentsen

LearningMatters

Acknowledgements

The authors would like to thank the following for their assistance with this book: Peter Kennard, Chrissie Coles, Dimitri Agejev, Dino Gomez and Emma Walkerdine.

First published in 2009 by Learning Matters Ltd

British Library Cataloguing in Publication Data
A CIP record for this book is available from the British Library.

ISBN: 978 1 84445 266 8

Cover design by Topics – The Creative Partnership
Text design by Code 5 Design Associates Ltd.
Project management by Diana Chambers
Typeset by Kelly Gray
Printed and bound in Great Britain by TJ International Ltd., Padstow, Cornwall

Learning Matters Ltd
33 Southernhay East
Exeter EX1 1NX
Tel: 01392 215560
info@learningmatters.co.uk
www.learningmatters.co.uk

FSC
Mixed Sources
Product group from well-managed forests and other controlled sources
Cert no. SGS-COC-2482
www.fsc.org
© 1996 Forest Stewardship Council

Contents

Introduction to the Written Exercises

The written exercises are an important part of the Police and PCSO recruitment process and appear to be something that candidates are quite concerned about. This may be because most people now use a computer or mobile phone to communicate with each other, rather than the more traditional paper and pen. As a result, some of the skills associated with the ability to write a memo, proposal or formal letter are not practised regularly. The thought of putting pen to paper without the benefit of spell-check (the F7 key) can be a challenging proposition for some. In addition, many have come to rely on those red and green squiggly lines highlighting spelling errors or poor grammar and making suggested changes to documents without perhaps stopping to think about what they have done incorrectly. Further, if you find that you can't think of a particular word, the combination of the Shift and F7 keys takes you to a thesaurus from which you can choose an appropriate word from a carefully selected list. You are no longer expected to think entirely for yourself and there is a tendency to take this technological wizardry for granted. That is, until the computer is no longer available and you realise that, without these support structures, the task of writing can be quite daunting. This is compounded during the assessment process, as it is coupled with the fear of making a mistake, in the knowledge that you are being tested. As a result, the process of written communication within the assessment centre can be a cause of anxiety for many.

This book is written to reduce that anxiety. It concentrates on just the written exercises and consists of three parts.

- Part 1 describes in detail how to prepare yourself for the assessment as it outlines the process and explains the rules of spelling, punctuation and grammar.

- Part 2 offers written exercises for you to practise.

- Part 3 offers a specimen response for each of the written exercises described in Part 2.

Part 1

Preparing for the assessment

OBJECTIVES

By the end of Part 1 you should be able to:

- identify the seven core competencies;

- explain the purpose of a written exercise;

- identify the four levels of competence;

- describe the process of the written exercise;

- recognise how to work wisely;

- recognise the mnemonic ICED;

- identify the general principles of written communication;

- explain the principles of spelling;

- explain the principles of punctuation;

- explain the principles of grammar;

- recognise the principles of reflective practice;

- engage in action planning;

- identify the SMART mnemonic;

- state the ten top tips for completing your written exercises.

The seven core competencies

You will be assessed against competencies that are relevant to the role of a police officer. What is a competency? A competency is a statement of how something should be done or performed. For example, *Supports arguments and recommendations effectively in writing*. It is observable and measurable and can be achieved by ensuring you reflect the advice provided within this book.

When your written work is assessed, consideration will be given to **what** you have written and **how** you have written it. The assessors will consider your written work in relation to the seven core competencies. A list of the competencies is shown below with a brief explanation of each (Cox, 2007).

1. Respect for race and diversity

Considers and shows respect for the opinions, circumstances and feelings of colleagues and members of the public, no matter what their race, religion, position, background, circumstances, status or appearance.

2. Team working

Develops strong working relationships inside and outside the team to achieve common goals. Breaks down barriers between groups and involves others in discussions and decisions.

3. Community and customer focus

Focuses on the customer and provides high-quality service that is tailored to meet their individual needs.

Understands the communities that are served and shows an active commitment to policing that reflects their needs and concerns.

4. Effective communication

Communicates ideas and information effectively, both verbally and in writing.

Uses language and a style of communication that is appropriate to the situation and people being addressed.

Makes sure that others understand what is going on.

5. Problem solving

Gathers information from a range of sources.

Analyses information to identify problems and issues and makes effective decisions.

6. Personal responsibility

Takes personal responsibility for making things happen and achieving results.

Displays motivation, commitment, perseverance and conscientiousness.

Acts with a high degree of integrity.

7. Resilience

Shows resilience, even in difficult circumstances.

Is prepared to make difficult decisions and has the confidence to see them through.

(Cox, 2007, p10)

For a full list of the positive and negative indicators associated with the National Core Competencies, see Appendix B.

The purpose of a written exercise

The purpose of the written exercises is to test your ability to communicate in writing. As a police officer you will be expected to record information accurately in a form that can be understood by others. Although information and communication technology (ICT) is gradually being introduced into the police service, there are occasions when your original notes are still written within a notebook, for example where an arrest has been made or an incident of note took place. Original notes are the record a police officer makes as soon as possible after an incident, during which time the details are still clear in his or her mind. These form the basis of a subsequent statement if a case is proceeded with to the appropriate court. This is often written many weeks or months after the original incident. Therefore, if the original notes are written poorly or certain words are illegible, mistakes could be made. A mistake made within the case papers can have the potential of losing a case. This is because it could throw an element of doubt on your honesty. A jury is reminded by the judge at the summing up stage of a case of what is referred to as the 'burden of proof'. In effect, this means that, if they have any doubt as to the person's guilt, they should find the accused not guilty.

When police officers take statements from witnesses, it is the practice that the officer records their account in paper form; therefore accuracy is paramount. Further, some reports, such as road traffic collision reports, are copied and forwarded to other interested parties; again it is essential that, as well as being accurate, the report is clear, coherent and comprehensive.

Other than making notes after an arrest, incident or collision, police officers are responsible for writing reports, replying to letters and recommending particular courses of action. For many of these, ICT is available, but a computer has its limitations. There are words that, although spelt correctly, may be used incorrectly, for example 'hours' is spelt as 'ours' or 'tours', etc., and because these words are spelt correctly the computer will not necessarily identify them. It is only with careful examination of the finished product that you will be able to identify these mistakes. For example, being able to recognise the difference between 'there', 'their' and 'they're' can assist your writing without the need to rely totally on the computer.

However, correct spelling alone does not ensure a well-structured piece of writing. The choice of words with which to express yourself is a good starting place. Then considerations of the order of those words in a sentence and the order of sentences in a paragraph will influence the readability of your work. It is not until you embark on a piece of writing that you begin to appreciate the characteristics of what you want to do. Suddenly, you can find that you have more questions than you have answers and you could find that you are less sure of what is required of you than you had previously thought.

Then there are further considerations.

- The recipient – who will be receiving your communication?

- The style – is your approach to be formal or informal?

- The level of familiarity – is it appropriate to be familiar with the person to whom you are writing?

- The beginning/end – how should you start and finish?

- The format – is there a set format for different types of writing, e.g. a memo, letter or proposal?

The purpose of the written exercise goes beyond just being able to spell correctly and construct a suitable piece of written work. You are also tested on your comprehension of a given situation and your ability to deal with a problem. This aspect will affect your final account or report, which will, in turn, affect your ability to solve a problem or deal with an issue. This is because you cannot solve a problem until you have identified what that problem actually is.

To this end the written exercise examines your:

- problem-solving skills;

- writing skills;

- grammar;

- spelling;

- communication.

The four levels of competence

It was suggested that, when you are tasked with writing, you could find yourself in a situation where you discover that you have more questions than you have answers. As a consequence, you could realise that you are less sure of what is required of you than you had previously thought. A representation of this is shown below in the form of a series of steps. These steps are commonly attributed to a person called Herzberg and so are known as Herzberg's Steps (Roffey-Barentsen and Malthouse, 2009). Here, four levels of competence are identified: from unconscious incompetence to unconscious competence.

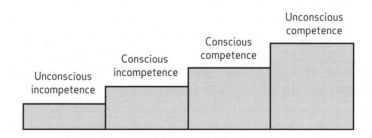

Step 1 Unconscious incompetence

This relates to a person who knows they have an assessment looming, but they have only just passed the first stage and have given little attention to the activities contained within the assessment because it feels such a long way off. They have simply no idea of what will be asked of them, they have given this no meaningful thought and they are described as being at the first step, that of 'unconscious incompetence'.

Step 2 Conscious incompetence

Later, the person is invited to attend an assessment centre. Now they decide to give attention to what is expected of them on the day. They research the topic by searching the Web, reading books and talking to others. Now they realise what they will be asked to do, but also realise that they may need to work hard on their spelling and grammar if they are to pass this element of the assessment. This person now stands on the second step referred to as 'conscious incompetence'. This is because they are aware that they may be lacking in ability at this stage.

Step 3 Conscious competence

After a while, the person has read up on the rules of spelling, grammar and constructing a report. They are conscious that they have difficulty with some aspects of the written exercise and are keen to ensure that they spell some words in particular correctly. They are aware that they need to check their work for careless mistakes and perhaps omissions. Here they have reached the next step, 'conscious competence'.

Step 4 Unconscious competence

Later, the person has now been writing at a certain standard for quite a while. The mistakes they once made have all but disappeared. Writing for them is no problem; they don't even have to think about it. They have reached the last step, 'unconscious competence'.

The implications for you as a learner

The useful thing about Herzberg's Steps is that you are giving some thought to your own ability. Thinking about how you are doing and what you may need to do to become more proficient is a very important aspect of your learning and progression. You may be asking yourself where you are now; if you are truthful to yourself, you will identify what you need to do to progress.

TASK 1

Consider the following question: 'For the purpose of the written exercise test, on which step is it appropriate to be?' The answers to all the tasks are given at the end of the book.

The written exercise process

During the assessment itself you can begin with any of the tests as you enter what is a form of carousel of activities. Before you embark on the written exercise the procedure will be explained to you. Don't be surprised if you find yourself in a room with other people who are also completing the written exercise. Paper and pens are provided and it will be obvious how to set out your work under the various titles. You do not enter your name on the form, but your candidate number.

What form do the written exercises take exactly? It is a contrived situation similar to the interactive exercises. In this case you are expected to assimilate information from a number of sources and create a memo or letter that is, in effect, a summary or précis of what you have read. Before starting the exercise you will be given a briefing sheet, which will include such information as who you are and what is expected of you. It will also explain the particular role that you will assume; typically you will be situated in a shopping centre. You will assume the role of a Customer Service Manager – a person who deals with people, their problems and issues; or a Security Guard Supervisor – a person responsible for the security guards at the centre.

The topics presented to you will vary from specific complaints to requests for a report on a topic where a recommendation is requested. You could be presented with varying points of view and will be expected to reflect these or allude to these within the body of your text.

The written assessment consists of two 20-minute exercises, during which candidates are required to read all the given documentation and to prepare a letter, memo or proposal. You will be told when you have five minutes remaining and then one minute remaining. Within the time provided you should do the following:

- read through the material;
- identify exactly what you have been asked to do;
- plan your writing;
- do your writing;
- check your work.

Read through the material

As you read through the material, make notes. These can be in the form of bullet points; you will not have the time to write long, detailed accounts of the situation. These notes will not be assessed. Order your bullet points so that you can see the relationships between things. Alternatively, a concept map can be useful (see below); this is where the information is placed on paper so that links can be made to the various aspects of the issue in hand. Don't spend too long on this stage, do only enough.

The concept map shown here indicates the things to be done and considered in preparation for the assessment. It does not matter what yours looks like, it just has to work for you. The advantage of a concept map is that it presents you with the overall picture; this can be useful as it ensures that you have gathered all the information available and that you don't forget anything in your report.

Identifying exactly what you have been asked to do

Having collated the information available, now go back and ask yourself exactly what you have been tasked with. Not answering the question would be a pity and can cost you marks. Having gleaned more information while reading the material, your task will become clearer.

Planning your writing

This need not take long and you may find that you have a good idea of the format of your written communication after having read through the material and made your notes. Making notes will inform your planning. This can take the form of what is known as the 'skeletal framework'; it identifies what needs doing, gives the overall structure and will remind you of the indicative content.

One thing to keep constantly in mind is your 'aim'; ask yourself what it is that you want to do exactly; what is this report all about? Identifying the aim will ensure that you have this at the back of your mind at all times, which will ensure that you do not go off track. Have you ever started writing and then realised you had lost the thread of what it was you were saying or where it was you were going to take the reader? If you write the aim down, you will be able to remind yourself constantly of what it is you want to achieve.

At the planning stage think about:

- the recipients of the communication;

- the points to include;

- the order in which the points should be made;

- the conclusion or recommendation(s);
- the general structure of your communication.

Producing your writing

Don't hang about, but don't rush either. This may sound contradictory, but the first thing to remember is that your time is very limited. You must make your decisions quickly, but these must be informed decisions, as there is no time to change your mind or procrastinate. You must get it right the first time. However, if you rush you will be inclined to make mistakes. Your handwriting will suffer and, as a consequence, the shape of your words will become less distinct. You may forget to dot your 'i's or cross your 't's, which could be interpreted as spelling mistakes. If you rush you are more likely to forget an important aspect of your proposal or argument. Keep your wits about you and ensure that you are aware of the time remaining. Remember, there are no extra marks for completing the written exercise, so if you feel you cannot complete the exercise, don't worry.

Checking your work

Although the written tests *assess your basic writing skills rather than your knowledge of the finer points of English Grammar* (Cox, 2007, p54), it is worth bearing in mind that, if you make five different spelling mistakes, you are likely to fail this task. However, once you spell a word incorrectly, subsequent spelling mistakes in that word will not be counted. What is wanted from you is to be able to *produce an example of writing that is legible, accurate and easy to understand* (ibid.).

Spell-checking

Throughout the book there will be exercises, called 'spell-checks', giving you the opportunity to check if you can spell some of the words that are commonly misspelt. It is important to ensure that you can spell these words. Ask a friend or relative to test you.

SPELL-CHECK

Learn the following words.

1. accidentally	5. maintenance	8. reference
2. accommodate	6. manoeuvre	9. relevant
3. acquire	7. referred	10. sandal
4. library		

Working wisely

Your work will be assessed for spelling, punctuation and grammar. So how can you guarantee that you will not make a spelling mistake? Being wise means that you only use words that you know how to spell and are confident to use. Using long complicated words is not at all impressive if the word you have used is spelt incorrectly. If you suddenly find that you are unsure how to spell a word, use another word or a combination of words to get around the problem. Working wisely means that you recognise how to use your spell-check. This takes the form of the written material that is presented to you for the purpose of the exercise. Here you will find many of the words that will be of use to you for your written exercise; copy these to your heart's content as you know they will be spelt correctly.

Punctuation and grammar can only be learned; there is no substitute, but you can learn the rules by reading books such as this one. You can also help yourself by reading a quality newspaper, journal or magazine. This will ensure that you experience a range of writing styles, helping you to recognise some principles of punctuation and grammar.

What is punctuation? According to **www.dictionary.com** (2008), it is *the practice or system of using certain conventional marks or characters in writing or printing in order to separate elements and make the meaning clear, as in ending a sentence or separating clauses.* But what is a clause? It is *a syntactic construction containing a subject and predicate and forming part of a sentence or constituting a whole simple sentence* (ibid.).

Herein lies the difficulty for a person trying to make sense of the specific terminology used to describe punctuation. In no time at all you end up asking more questions than you started with. You don't need to know the definitions of, for example, punctuation or grammar to be able to do them, although it certainly helps. And, as you may be wondering what grammar is, it is *the study of the way the sentences of a language are constructed; morphology and syntax* (ibid.). So now that is cleared up we can move on . . . or perhaps not.

A more approachable description may be that punctuation concerns things such as full stops at the end of a sentence and the use of question marks, apostrophes, commas, etc., and grammar is the way the words in a sentence are used in combination. Punctuation and grammar form part of the rules; your task is to grasp the rules so that you can pass the written exercise and become a police officer.

The mnemonic ICED

A mnemonic is something that is used to assist your memory. In this instance, the letters ICED form a word designed to trigger your memory to be able to remember other specific words. This mnemonic is designed to assist you in structuring your writing. The following example shows how it can be employed.

I Introduction	Briefly **introduce** the report.
	This report considers the parking in Ashford Road, which is presenting a danger to pedestrians.
C Circumstances	Explain the **circumstances**.
	The parking in Ashford Road is causing problems for both road users and pedestrians. Cars are being left on the grass verge that runs parallel to the kerb. The effect of this is that the

verge is being eroded by constant use of the vehicles. Pedestrians, especially those who attempt to cross the road at this point with children, have reported difficulty when negotiating around the cars with pushchairs or prams. The road is private and, therefore, does not benefit from the attention of the local authorities.

E Effective interventions

Describe the various **effective interventions** available.

If we do not intervene effectively, I believe that serious injury will result. To prevent this the following can be considered.

1. *A member of the security staff is utilised to patrol the area. The effect of this will be to dissuade members of the public from parking their vehicles on the verge.*

2. *Signs are to be placed in the vicinity, the effect of which will be to urge motorists not to park and to warn pedestrians of the associated dangers of crossing the road at that point.*

3. *Concrete barriers are placed on the verge with the effect of preventing parking.*

D Decision

State the details of any proposed **decision** and conclude with a proposal.

Option 1 will be expensive and effective for as long as a security guard is available.

Option 2 will be expensive and ineffectual, as experience has indicated that people tend to ignore signs that are not obviously enforceable.

Option 3 is expensive but effective.

I propose that the installation of physical barriers is the only effective option to prevent parking and, subsequently, injury to members of the public.

(Reproduced with kind permission of
The Interview Success Company Ltd, 2009)

This example is brief, but shows how the ICED mnemonic is employed – it is easy to remember and its simplicity is key to its success. Alternatively, you can design your own mnemonic to suit your specific needs.

The advantage of structuring your communication is that, rather than the information being presented in no particular order, here you think about what you want to say, organise your thoughts and present them in a way that is appropriate for the reader. If it helps, ask yourself what you would want to know if you were the reader of your written work.

SPELL-CHECK

Learn the following words.

11. acceptable	15. millennium	18. rhythm
12. acquit	16. miniature	19. schedule
13. amateur	17. ridiculous	20. scissors
14. memento		

The general principles of written communication

Written communication should be clear, concise and accurate.

- *Clear*

  Clarity is achieved by appropriate planning. During the planning stage of your preparation it is useful to ask yourself the following.

  - Have I identified the purpose of the communication?

  - Have I decided what to tell my reader in order to achieve this?

  - Have I laid my facts down in a clear and logical sequence?

  - Have I checked the message from my reader's point of view?

- *Concise*

  Only use as many words as you need to convey the message you are communicating. Don't use unnecessary words or phrases with a large number of words if a much shorter phrase will do. Consider every word and decide whether it adds to the message or not.

- *Accurate*

  You are being tested on your knowledge based upon your reading of the material presented to you. Do not assume anything or add to the material in any way; your communication must be accurate. Know your facts.

Words

Words are the basic elements for all written communication. Choose your words with care and remember that, often, the subtle differences in the meanings of words are very fine. Words are assembled together in sentences.

Sentences

Ideally, you should aim to have an average sentence length of about 15 words. This is short enough to be clear and long enough for the wording to flow well. Try to vary the length of your sentences to make your writing more interesting. Sentences are grouped together into paragraphs.

Paragraphs

Paragraphs should have a common theme, topic or idea. They are especially useful to allow the reader to pause and think about what they have just read. Paragraphs structure your argument. The number of paragraphs in a piece of written work will depend on its length.

Tools

You, the writer, shape your words, sentences and paragraphs with the aid of three tools: spelling, grammar and punctuation. This book will now consider these topics. It will set you various tasks along the way, so that your learning is more interactive and therefore measurable.

The principles of spelling

When it comes to spelling we offer three rules.

The three rules of spelling
1. Don't make spelling mistakes.
2. Don't make spelling mistakes.
3. Don't make spelling mistakes.

This advice is given to you on the basis that you may write a fantastic report, beautifully laid out with correct punctuation reflecting the rules of grammar. But, if your spelling lets you down, that's it, you fail the assessment.

Spelling is one of the few features of written communication that is not a matter of personal opinion; it is fact and is either right or wrong. Your ability to spell is assessed in written exercises. There is no short cut to spelling; either you know it or you don't and, if you don't, then you have to learn how to spell certain words or choose not to use them. Many people have a few tricks up their sleeves when it comes to spelling words they are unsure of. Techniques such as masking can be very useful. Masking means that, if you cannot remember whether the 'i' comes before the 'e', then both the 'i' and the 'e' are looped so they become indistinguishable and the dot that should go over the 'i' is placed very carefully exactly between the two loops. Alternatively, you can make your handwriting very messy, implying that you were in a great hurry and, although you knew how to spell the word, you didn't have time to write it in full. These tricks, which may have carried you through your previous examinations, letters and various communications, will not be appropriate for the written exercise. If your writing is not legible (if it cannot be read) then you will be marked accordingly. Bad spelling gives a bad impression.

TASK 2

Identify the spelling mistakes in the following sentence.

The police service of the twenty-first centery relys on the willingness of the communitties too be policed.

Dealing with plurals

The following rules consider spelling in terms of:

- simple plurals;

- mutated plurals;

- nouns that are the same when plural;

- nouns that are never singular.

Simple plurals

To make a word a plural you usually add an '**s**' to it (not an apostrophe then an 's'), e.g. dog**s**, sofa**s**, shoe**s**, book**s**.

Nouns (words used to name a person, place, thing, quality or action) that end in a hissing sound (sibilant) need '**es**' to be added to them when they are used as a plural, that is unless they already end in an '**e**', e.g. bus**es**, class**es**, wish**es**, siz**es**.

If there is a vowel (a, e, i, o, u) before the last '**y**' in a word, add an '**s**' to make the word plural, e.g. key – key**s**, bay – bay**s**.

However, if there is a consonant (every letter that is not a vowel) before the '**y**', the '**y**' gets changed to and '**i**' and then you add '**es**', e.g. berry – berr**ies**; century – centur**ies**.

Mutated plurals

Some words change internally when they become plurals; these are known as 'mutated plurals'. There are only a few that come up in everyday language and that need to be learnt:

child   –   children
die   –   dice
foot   –   feet
man   –   men
penny   –   pence
tooth   –   teeth
woman   –   women.

SPELL-CHECK

Learn the following words.

21. apparent	25. mischievous	28. vacuum
22. argument	26. noticeable	29. vicious
23. atheist	27. occasion	30. weather
24. believe		

Nouns that are the same when plural

There are a few words that remain in the same form whether they are singular or plural, e.g.:

aircraft   forceps
deer   salmon
series   sheep.

Nouns that are never singular

Another set of nouns are those that are never singular. These are listed for you to learn:

binoculars	pincers
eaves	pliers
measles	scissors
news	spectacles
pants	trousers.

TASK 3

Complete the following sentences, adding 's', 'es' or 'ies' to the underlined words as you think appropriate:

1. She found the police <u>officer</u> were very helpful.

2. As she searched the house, she noticed the room was full of <u>toy</u> for <u>baby</u>.

3. 'I am getting fed up with all these <u>tax</u>,' the inspector complained.

4. Of all the capital <u>city</u>, London is my favourite.

5. As you look over the rooftops towards Hampton Court, you can see hundreds of <u>chimney</u>.

6. The sun's <u>ray</u> burst through the clouds like fingers pointing at the ground.

Underline the words used incorrectly.

7. She was a petite women.

8. He said that all of his tooths hurt.

9. The aircrafts were screaming across the sky.

10. He was using his binocular to see the deers.

Placing letters in words

The following rules consider spelling in terms of:

- placing '**f**', '**l**' and '**s**' at the end of a word – the flossy word rule;

- placing '**i**' before '**e**' or '**e**' before '**i**';

- placing '**all**', '**full**' and '**till**' next to a word;

- placing '**er**' or '**or**' at the end of a word.

Flossy word rule

With short words ending in '**f**', '**l**' and '**s**' (hence flossy), double that letter after a short vowel, e.g. staff, cross, shall, fuss, yell.

'ei' and 'ie'

You may be familiar with the phrase, 'i before e, except after c, whenever it rhymes with me'. This is a useful rule to remember, but beware of exceptions, such as the word 'seize'.

'i' before 'e'	Except after 'c'
chief	ceiling
field	deceive
yield	receive
shield	deceit
priest	conceive

'all', 'full' and 'till'

When 'all', 'full' and 'till' are joined to a word, or part of a word, they drop an 'l', e.g. also, hopeful, until, always, altogether, almost.

'er' and 'or'

Both 'er' and 'or' endings are found in words that describe what people do, e.g. banker, gaoler, tailor, director.

In words that describe what things do, 'or' is the more common ending, e.g. detonator, refrigerator, incubator. There are exceptions, though, most notably computer.

TASK 4

Underline the spelling mistakes.

1. It's as I said; you know I allways tell the truth, well allmost. I may have had a gun in my hand standing outside the bank, officor. But I had no idea there was an armed robbery taking place inside the bank; there was quite a fus. In fact, I found the gun on the floor and was going to hand it to you. Luckily you came around the corner, found me and siezed the gun.

2. I was told that, if I wanted to recieve less spam, I would have to place a cross in the box.

3. You don't deceive me; you have hidden the money by carefully taping each note to the cieling and then painting over it.

4. I was hopefull that we would be able to get together, all of us, in the house on the hill, but it was alltogether too difficult.

5. The house on the hill, you say? I was allso looking forward to it until I heard that a plane allmost came through the roof. That's what happens when you leave the landing light on.

6. I don't know what I should do for a living. Allthough I could be a police officer, teacher, tax collecter or racing driver, I might prefer being a person of leisure.

7. That sounds wonderfull!

SPELL-CHECK

Learn the following words.

31. calendar	35. occurrence	38. weird
32. category	36. official	39. quiet
33. cemetery	37. quite	40. tyranny
34. occur/occurred		

Adding letters (suffixes) to words

The following rules consider spelling in terms of:

- adding '**ing**' to words;

- adding '**and**' and '**ent**' to words;

- adding '**y**' to words;

- adding '**able**' and '**ible**' to words;

- adding '**sion**' and '**tion**' to words.

'*ing*'

There are rules for adding '**ing**' to a verb (an action word). It is useful to remember that some do not change, e.g.:

catching	talking
eating	teaching
trying	crying
sleeping	fishing.

After a short vowel, double the consonant before adding '**ing**'. The consonant is the letter that is not a vowel, e.g.:

run	–	running
shop	–	shopping
dig	–	digging.

If the verb ends in '**e**', take it off before adding '**ing**', e.g.:

take	–	taking
complete	–	completing
hope	–	hoping.

If a word ends in '**ie**', change it to '**y**' before adding '**ing**', e.g.:

tie	–	tying
lie	–	lying.

17

'ant' and 'ent'

Words ending in 'ant' and 'ent' are among the most commonly misspelt words, so if you are not entirely sure that you are using them correctly, now is the time to check them before the day at the assessment centre. There is no rule for the types of words that end in 'ant' and 'ent'. But there is a rule that words ending in 'ance' will always be formed from words that end in 'ant', in the same way that words ending in 'ence' come from words ending in 'ent', e.g.:

predominant – predominance
different – difference.

'y'

The letter 'y' usually comes at the end of a word. When you add an ending *except* 'ing', change the 'y' to an 'i', e.g.:

	Adding 'es'	Adding 'ed'	Adding 'ing'
carry	carries	carried	carrying
hurry	hurries	hurried	hurrying
supply	supplies	supplied	supplying.

'able' and 'ible'

This is another problem for some and here the rule is: if the part of the word before the ending is complete, the end will be 'able', e.g.:

know – knowable
read – readable.

If the part of the word before the ending is not complete, the ending will be 'ible', e.g.:

permiss – permissible
ed – edible.

'sion' and 'tion'

Words ending in 'sion' and 'tion' are usually nouns that are formed from verbs. A noun is a word that is used to name a person, place or thing, e.g. woman, seaside, chair. A verb is a word that expresses existence, action or occurrence, e.g. live, run, stop.

Nouns ending in 'sion' are formed from verbs ending in:

Examples	Verb	Noun ('sion')
nd	expand	expansion
de	provide	provision
ss	discuss	discussion
mit	omit	omission
pel	propel	propulsion
vert	divert	diversion.

Nouns ending in 'tion' are formed from verbs ending in:

Examples	Verb	Noun ('tion')
ct	act	action
te	create	creation
ise	organise	organisation
ose	suppose	supposition
erve	reserve	reservation.

When the sound is 'shun', never write 'sh', except for 'fashion' and 'cushion'. Nearly all the others end with '**tion**'.

TASK 5

Add '**ing**' to the following words, making any necessary changes to the original word.

1. try
2. cry
3. shoplift
4. chop

5. roll
6. escape
7. make

8. steal
9. lie
10. untie

TASK 6

Add either '**ance**' or '**ence**' to the end of the following words, making any necessary changes.

1. arrogant
2. resistant
3. silent
4. obedient

5. absent
6. distant
7. intolerant

8. belligerent
9. impatient
10. radiant

TASK 7

One word has been used incorrectly within some of the following sentences. Identify the *incorrect* sentences and offer an alternative word.

1. I carried the water. Correct/Incorrect?
   Alternative spelling _____

2. I love curry'ed eggs. Correct/Incorrect?
   Alternative spelling _____

3. Blackberries are wonderful. Correct/Incorrect?
   Alternative spelling _____

4. Once I supplyed all the police stations with blue lights. Correct/Incorrect?
   Alternative spelling _____

TASK 7 *continued*

The following words finish with 'able' or 'ible'. Underline those that you think have been used *incorrectly*.

5. comfortable
6. visable
7. predictable
8. understandible
9. flexible

Underline the words among the following that are spelt *incorrectly*.

10. action
11. reservasion
12. discussion
13. nation
14. organisasion
15. divertion

SPELL-CHECK

Learn the following words.

41. changeable	45. questionnaire	48. restaurant
42. column	46. receive	49. sensible
43. committed	47. religious	50. separate
44. privilege		

Homonyms and homophones

The following rules consider spelling in terms of:

- homonyms;

- homophones.

Homonyms

Homonyms are words that have the same spelling but have different meanings. The word is made from two Greek words, 'homos' meaning 'same' and 'onoma' meaning 'name'. So 'homonym' means 'of the same name'. Sometimes homonyms are pronounced differently, and sometimes they sound the same, e.g.:

row – to row a boat
row – to argue
row – a row of soldiers.

Other common homonyms include the following:

lead   the metal, or the thing you walk a dog with

reading   the place, or the action of reading a book

sow   to scatter seed, or the name for a female pig

tear   a rip in a piece of paper or fabric, or something people shed when they are very sad.

It is unlikely that homonyms will cause you any trouble with your spelling because the spelling is the same, unlike homophones.

Homophones

Homophones are words that sound the same but are spelt differently and have different meanings. The word is made from two Greek words, 'homos' meaning 'same' and 'phone' meaning 'sound'. So 'homophone' means 'same sound'. These can be confusing, so to be sure you are using the correct spelling of a word it is beneficial if you learn the word in its context. The following is one example.

On that day the rain was persistent and heavy.

Queen Victoria's reign spanned two centuries.

TASK 8

There are 18 incorrectly used homophones in this passage. See if you can identify them.

As a Police Community Support Officer, I can't weight two see the fare, as it brings out the best in the local people. I hope it is as good as last year. I was off duty at the time and remember that won ride hurt me so much, it gave me a pane in my side, witch lasted up too a weak. I will sea if the bumper cars are in the same plaice; it would be nice to meat up their again. Although, if eye remember correctly, they maid me feel a little sick. I think the fair is grate. What do yew think; am I rite or knot?

TASK 9

Place the correct word in its place within the sentence.

1. grate/great
   To make a _____ cauliflower cheese you will have to _____ a lot of cheese.

2. made/maid
   Although the cook _____ the sandwiches, the _____ served them.

3. mail/male
   It was not uncommon for the _____ members of the cast to receive vast amounts of
   _____.

TASK 9 *continued*

4. more/moor
   Even _____ birds were found to be nesting on the _____ .

5. been/bean
   He looked down at his plate where the last _____ had _____ .

Commonly confused words

The following rules consider spelling in terms of:

- to, too and two;

- there, their and they're;

- the use of 'was'.

to, too and two

Three words that are often confused are 'to', 'too' and 'two'. If you think of the word 'to' as in 'going to the zoo', for example, then, if the zoo is a long way away, you could say 'it is too far away'. If you are lucky when you get there, there may be 'two zoos for the price of one'. The example below shows the words used in their different forms. They all sound alike, which is the problem for many.

The two words that are confused all too often cause me to wince.

there, their and they're

Again, it is the homophones that are causing the problems. Homophones are words that, although they are spelt differently, sound the same. The example below shows the words used in their different forms.

There are always people who think they're in the park for their dogs' exercise.

The three forms of this word are:

- **there**, denoting place, for example 'over there' or 'she is there on the motorcycle';

- **their**, as in belonging to them, for example 'their motorcycles';

- **they're**, formed from two words, they and are, hence the apostrophe; this denotes a contraction, showing that something has been omitted, for example 'they're always in the way' or 'they're never going to make it'.

Homophones are commonly found in humorous passages or jokes; when this occurs people refer to 'a play on words', e.g.:

Customer	Waiter, what kind of soup is this?
Waiter	It's bean soup, sir.
Customer	I don't care what it has been; what is it now?

Use of 'was'

Some people are using the word 'was' in place of the word 'were'. Often the way in which a person speaks is reflected in the way they write, and an awareness of this can prevent what could have been unfortunate and even unconscious mistakes, e.g.:

Incorrect use	Correct use
You was coming to my house.	You were coming to my house.
You was lying.	You were lying.
You was never going to make it on time.	You were never going to make it on time.

SPELL-CHECK

Learn the following words.

51. conscience
52. conscientious
53. conscious
54. occasionally

55. parallel
56. parliament
57. pastime

58. success
59. tomorrow
60. twelfth

Plurals revisited

Plurals are the one aspect of the written exercise that appears to cause the most problems for many people. Therefore, this subject is revisited in more detail.

Using 's' or 'es'

As you are aware, to make most words plural (where there is more than one of something), all you do is add an 's'.

The golden rule is not to use what is commonly referred to as the greengrocer's apostrophe, just to make a plural, e.g.:

Potatoe's, cabbage's and pea's all 50 per cent off.

The exceptions to the rule of just adding an 's' are, first, the plurals of words ending in an 'o'. These words can end in either an 's' or an 'es'.

The other exceptions are words that end in 'ch', 'sh', 's', 'ss', 'x' or 'z'. With words ending in these letters, you make the plural by adding 'es'.

Still with plurals, we consider words ending in 'f' or 'fe', e.g.:

wife – wives
scarf – scarves
thief – thieves
loaf – loaves.

What do you notice about the way in which these words become plural? These words, when in their plural form, change the way in which they are spelt: the '**f**' becomes a '**v**'. Other words, such as 'mouse' to 'mice', change even more noticeably; this is an example of a mutated plural.

Remember, some words don't change at all when they become plural, such as 'salmon', 'trout' or 'pike'. Out of interest, if you have more than one fish, is it 'fish' or 'fishes'? (The answer is below.) Other animals that make an appearance under this category are sheep, deer and buffalo. Then there are series, aircraft and offspring.

Finally, there are words that are only used in the plural form, even when they refer to a word in the singular, for example 'headquarters' and 'barracks'.

TASK 10

Decide which, if any, of the following are correct.

1. It's two hot in here.
2. It takes too to tango.
3. Two many crooks spoil the bank job.
4. One, two, three, four.
5. They're going to get cold up there.
6. Over their, look.
7. By the looks of things, they're busy.
8. I was right, they're in the cell.
9. You was right, their all out.
10. Two was the answer, but that was before one ran off.

State the plural of the following words.

11. beach   –   _____
12. tax   –   _____
13. patch   –   _____
14. bus   –   _____
15. palace   –   _____
16. knife   –   _____
17. leaf   –   _____
18. sheep   –   _____
19. half   –   _____
20. mouse   –   _____

(Answer to 'fish' or 'fishes'? In fact, either 'fish' or 'fishes' is correct, although 'fish' is probably the most common these days.)

SPELL-CHECK

Learn the following words.

61. definite
62. disappear
63. discipline
64. drunkenness

65. embarrass
66. pigeon
67. possession

68. preferable
69. precede
70. recommend

The principles of punctuation

The aim of punctuation is to clarify the wording for the reader. While words and their groupings into sentences and paragraphs are the raw materials of written communication, punctuation is probably the most important of the tools. A well-constructed, logical piece of written work, composed with carefully chosen words, can be distorted beyond recognition or made totally incomprehensible by inadequate or incorrect punctuation. Consider the following.

I can't think how to go about it your way.

I can't think how to, go about it your way.

I can't, think how to go about it your way.

By inserting commas in the same sentence, each sentence reads differently. It's important that you use punctuation to help your reader make sense of your writing. If you talked to them, they would be helped by pauses, the rise and fall of your voice and changes in emphasis. In writing, however, punctuation performs some of these functions. If the punctuation you use causes any doubt as to the meaning of the passage, it could be that your punctuation marks are wrongly chosen or wrongly placed.

Full stop (.)

A full stop should be used to end a sentence. Unfortunately, many people tend to use commas when they should use full stops, which has the effect of running two or more sentences together. This not only reads very badly, but will mean that you will be marked down in the written test. If you are unsure of how to use a full stop, you can use them to split your writing into manageable chunks, indicating to your reader when they should pause.

Comma (,)

Your writing style will often determine how you use commas. Use them to make the meaning clearer, e.g.:

In my opinion there is every reason to suspect the vicar, with the candlestick, in the lounge.

Or use them to form a list within a sentence, e.g.:

> The ingredients include butter, flour, sugar and a very large quantity of chocolate.

Remember, when writing a list, that there is no need to use a comma before the last item, unless leaving it out would make the meaning unclear.

Semi-colon (;)

Semi-colons can be used instead of full stops to separate two closely related statements, e.g.:

> Britain and the Netherlands are monarchies; the United States of America and France have a president as head of state.

They can also be used to combine two ideas into one sentence, where *The first idea leads to the second one but they are both important* (Hickey, 2008, p84), e.g.:

> The parking situation in the Dudley Road is causing problems for pedestrians; before long someone is going to be seriously injured or killed.

The semi-colon is also used in contrasting statements, e.g.:

> I want to be a police officer; he a teacher.

> My favourite colour is pink; hers blue.

Sometimes, a semi-colon is used in a list within a sentence where the listed items consist of several words, e.g.:

> The experiences of the respondents are: not being kept informed of progress; high costs; low standards; and a general lack of enthusiasm from staff.

Colon (:)

The colon's main uses are to introduce a list or series, or a quotation, e.g.:

> The ingredients include:
> - butter
> - flour
> - sugar
> - a very large quantity of chocolate.

The author of the book said:

> *The colon has two main uses: to introduce a list or series, or to introduce a quotation.*

Apostrophe (')

Many appear unsure of when to use an apostrophe, but it is highly likely that it will occur during your written exercise. Use apostrophes to show possession of something. Add an apostrophe to the person or object having possession, e.g.:

> The police officer's uniform.

> The assessment centre's decision.

If there is more than one person doing the possessing and the word already ends in 's', add an apostrophe after the 's', e.g.:

Five officers' uniforms.

However, if you are using someone's name, you will need to add 's', even if the name ends with an 's', e.g.:

Charles's uniform.

And do the same when a noun ends in 'ss', e.g.:

The boss's uniform.

You can also use an apostrophe to show where letters have been left out, e.g.:

it's (it is)

don't (do not)

the sky's the limit (the sky is the limit).

Be aware of a common mistake with the word 'could've'. Commonly, candidates are misrepresenting the words by lengthening it to read 'could of', whereas the second part of the word represents the word 'have'. Thus, 'I could have done that' becomes 'I could've done that.'

Pronouns (words used instead of a noun), such as 'hers', 'ours', 'yours' and 'its', do not need apostrophes, e.g.:

The concert reached its climax.

Exclamation mark (!)

Exclamation marks are used after an exclamation, such as Wow! or Hey! They are also used for commands. It is, therefore, highly unlikely that you will need to use one in your writing during the written exercise.

Question mark (?)

Use question marks only when you are asking a direct question, e.g.:

What is the situation with the maintenance of the CCTV?

Do not use them like this:

I am writing to ask you what the situation is with the maintenance of the CCTV?

This is not a direct question and, therefore, does not need a question mark.

Inverted commas (")

You may use inverted commas for:

• direct quotations, e.g.: She said, 'A large hole has been found in the High Street; the police are looking into it';

- nicknames, e.g.: 'Ali' Falconer – this makes it clear that Ali is a nickname;

- book titles, report titles, etc.

You should not use them for:

- jargon;

- technical phrases;

- emphasis – as in drawing attention to an off-the-wall work or humorous phrase.

Capital letters

You will need to use a capital letter at the start of each sentence and for proper names, such as Thomas, Ela or Vindi, but consider this example:

> One of the chief inspectors is Chief Inspector Bell.

A good rule to remember is – if you are talking generally, use lower case. If you are being specific, use capitals (upper case). In this example, 'chief inspector' is general, while 'Chief Inspector Bell' is specific.

Parenthesis (brackets or dashes)

This sounds more complicated than it is. You probably already use parenthesis, which is an extra piece of information included in a sentence. If the additional part is removed, the sentence will still make sense (Hickey, 2008). The following examples use brackets or dashes:

> *Soon after the Long Winter began, and Rohan lay under snow for nearly five months (November to March 2758–9).*
>
> (Tolkien, 1988, p347)

> *The middle section of the driver's number – 706132 – is formulated from the holder's date of birth. The first and last digits – the 7 and 2 – relate to the year of birth, so in this case the driver was born in 1972.*
>
> (Madsen, 2007, p24)

The above examples are considered strong forms of parenthesis, so wherever possible use commas because they are less likely to interrupt your reader's flow, e.g.:

> *There was a white horse, on a quiet winter morning when snow covered the streets gently and was not deep, and the sky was swept with vibrant stars, except in the east, where dawn was beginning in a light blue flood.*
>
> (Helprin, 1983, p3)

This concludes the basics of the rules of punctuation, but there are other aspects that may influence your writing. These are identified in the next section, which considers the principles of grammar.

The principles of grammar

Grammar covers sentence structure, word order and many other more specialised aspects, such as tense and agreement.

Common grammatical pitfalls

Recent trends in writing allow us to break some of the rules of grammar. It will help you to be aware of some of the pitfalls that are common in report and memo writing, so that you will be fully prepared for your assessment.

Disagreement of noun/pronoun/verb

Before we look at disagreements, it may be useful to consider what nouns, pronouns and verbs are.

- Noun   Word used as a name of a person, place or thing.
- Pronoun   Word used in place of a noun, e.g. her, our, your.
- Verb   A word that describes the occurrence or performance of an action. A 'doing' word.

Let's look at a sentence. What's wrong with it?

A pan as well as a cooker are necessary.

Consider which word is the subject of the sentence. 'A pan' is the subject of the sentence and is singular. Therefore 'are' should be changed to 'is':

A pan as well as a cooker is necessary.

Word order

Consider the following:

Three Australian nationals, just released from prison in Sierra Leone, gave a horrifying account of torture and appalling conditions that they had suffered when they arrived at Sydney Airport.

The sentence is misleading and highlights the importance of word order. Written this way, it appears that the torture occurred at Sydney Airport. Another way of ordering the information could be:

On their arrival at Sydney Airport, four Australian nationals gave horrifying accounts of the torture and appalling conditions they had suffered while in prison in Sierra Leone.

Tautology

The term 'tautology' means to repeat the same meaning, using different words, e.g.:

repeat again	new innovation
free gift	lonely isolation
in this day and age	widow woman.

Reflective practice

The following pages are dedicated to practice in the written exercises. After you have completed each one, it is recommended that you undertake what is referred to as reflective practice (Malthouse et al., 2009). You can do this by asking yourself four things.

1. What did I do?

2. How well did I do it?

3. What does this book suggest I should have done?

4. What will I do differently in future?

Having identified these you can devise an Action Plan.

You can find the form below to do this (if it helps you can photocopy it to use). You don't need anyone else to tell you how you did, as the beauty of reflective practice is that you know how well you did and, if you are honest with yourself, you will know in which areas you need to do more work.

Question 3 above can be easily answered. In Part 3 of this book an example of a suitable response for each of the exercises is included. Comparing this with your own efforts will benefit you and prepare you for doing even better on the next occasion.

Reflective Practice Sheet

Title	Your observations
1. What did I do?	
2. How well did I do it?	
3. What does this book say I should have done?	
4. What will I do differently in future?	Desired outcome:
5. Action Plan	S M A R T

Reflective practice is all about taking responsibility for your own efforts in an attempt to improve whatever it is you are doing. You are the person who knows best what you can do well and what needs improving, so arguably it is you who is best placed to decide what requires improvement. You will notice from the Reflective Practice Sheet that the reflective process consists of four parts or phases. The first part asks 'What did I do?' Thinking about what happened is always a good place to start the process. At this stage you think about the written exercise, remembering as much as you can about the preparation, your ability to read the material, your use of time, etc. For example, you could ask yourself:

- 'Did I read the information thoroughly?'

- 'Did I identify all the salient points?'

- 'Did I plan what I was going to write?'

- 'Did I make best use of the time available?'

- 'Did I get stuck?'

- 'Did I use only the words I could spell?'

- 'Did I structure the writing appropriately?'

As you ask yourself these questions, try to remember how you felt as you completed each part of the written exercise. The feeling that you have messed it up is a common one and is associated with demanding the very best from yourself. During the written exercise you may feel that you wish to scrap what you have done and just start again. You look at the mistakes you have crossed out and perhaps feel that the mess in front of you will never pass the assessor's critical eye. Sometimes you may feel that you have made a mistake and that you have failed the assessment. The analogy is a little like taking a driving test during which you make a mistake. You feel sure that you have failed and, as a result, your driving deteriorates, your concentration drops and you chastise yourself for making the mistake. But, at that moment, you had not failed. Unfortunately, your driving is poor due to you being so hard on yourself and you are in danger of failing. Why? Because you have decided you have – there is no other reason than that. There is the danger of creating a self-fulfilling prophecy. The same can happen in the assessment centre where you make a mistake and you cannot put it behind you. If you dwell on it you will disadvantage yourself. The best policy is to put the experience behind you and move on, having learned from it.

The second part of your reflective practice considers the question 'How well did I do it?' You don't need anyone else to tell you where you found it difficult or where you felt that it was going well. What is important here is that you consider the written exercise from your own point of view. Being honest with yourself will mean that you can admit that there are areas of your performance that will benefit from further attention. At this stage you could ask yourself:

> 'Did I read the information thoroughly?' – No, I missed one thing out that I only managed to notice when I was checking through the report. At that stage I only had about two minutes to make amends.

> 'Did I identify all the salient points?' – Yes, at least at first I thought I had, and then I realised later that I had missed the significance of a particular sentence and so had to try to fit it in. This made the appearance of the written word messy and I was not too happy with that.

> 'Did I plan what I was going to write?' – Yes, I found the concept map really useful and I could see on one page the whole situation as it appeared to me.

'Did I make best use of the time available?' – No, not really. I must try to read more quickly and do the preparation so that I have time to do the writing. It seems unfair that, although I could explain it to someone, I have to write it down.

'Did I get stuck?' – No, I was too busy to get stuck and I think the only place you can get stuck is at the start, where you are trying to make sense of everything.

'Did I use only the words I could spell?' – Yes, and by copying the words from the information that I was given. It feels a bit like cheating, but it works for me.

'Did I structure the writing appropriately?' – Yes, the form I was given showed me where to put my number and indicated where to write. I think I expressed myself well and ensured that all aspects of the work were considered.

The difference between parts 1 and 2 of the process is that, at part 1, you ask yourself if you did something and, at part 2, you ask yourself how well you did it.

Having done that, you are ready for stage 3, which asks 'What does this book suggest I should have done?' A specimen written answer is provided at the end of the book. Think about this and ask yourself how it compares to what you have done. This part of the process is designed to offer you other possibilities – other ways of expressing yourself and structuring the written work. It offers different perspectives and is designed to simulate the role of a personal coach.

The last question, 4, asks 'What will I do differently in future?' You are best placed to answer this, as by now you will have thought about what you have written, reflected upon how you did and read the specimen response to identify what else you could have written. Try to state your desired outcome in one sentence, as that way it is easier to recognise. Now it is time for your Action Plan – here you identify exactly what you are going to do differently next time.

Action planning

An Action Plan is a statement of intention to arrive at a specific outcome or goal. The goal is more likely to be achieved if it is properly thought through and planned and if the person has an active interest in achieving the goal. In other words, if you decide for yourself what you want to achieve, you will be more likely to achieve that goal than if some other person was to set the goal for you. In general, people have a tendency to procrastinate – they put off doing things in favour of other things that are more fun or involve less effort. Action planning is relatively easy. It is the 'Action' that takes the effort.

An Action Plan should be SMART. That means it must be:

- **S**pecific
- **M**easurable
- **A**chievable
- **R**elevant
- **T**imed.

The Reflective Practice Sheet (see page 30) has been designed to incorporate this concept as part 5 of the process, as shown in the example below.

Desired outcome: To speed up my reading when preparing

5. Action Plan	**Specific:** To spend less time preparing the written exercise.
	Measurable: To spend no more than five minutes in preparation.
	Achievable: This is achievable if I think about what I am doing and practise it.
	Relevant: This is relevant to the written exercises.
	Timed: To be completed within five days.

Advice from other people, for example a member of your family, or another person who has experience of writing at this level, will of course be useful and that may assist you. However, although they can point out any spelling, grammatical or punctuation errors, they will only be able to offer advice on the finished product. You, though, will be aware of the process, and what you had to experience to achieve what you did. Other people will often be talking from their own perspective and not your own. They may not recognise how you felt at the time, what you were thinking, what you were not thinking, what you found most difficult, how it was for you, etc. Only you know that, and as a result only you can decide exactly how and what you are going to do that makes sense for you.

The process of reflective practice is a very personal one. The great thing about it is that it actually works. To make it work for you, you must first be honest with yourself and listen to your own advice. Remember, if you always do what you always did, you will always get what you always got.

Frequently asked questions: some common concerns

Below are a few questions and answers that relate to the completion of the exercises.

'As I do the exercises in the book, if I am unsure of how to spell a word, should I look it up or is that cheating?'

The answer is, if you have realised that you can't spell a word, look it up in a dictionary, visit **www.dictionary.com** or write the word you are unsure of using a computer program to identify whether it is spelt correctly. Being aware of the fact that you do not know something is a part of the learning process.

'I am worried about my spellings, so what can I do about it?'

There is no short cut to spelling, so your task is to use the words that you know you know and don't even think about using any others at the assessment centre. It is up to you – if you feel you want to improve your vocabulary, you must go about learning to spell the words correctly. During the assessment, you are all on your own; there will be no one to ask and no IT to help you, so you have the time now to learn those words – use it wisely.

'I am dyslexic; what help can I get with the written work?'

If you are dyslexic, it is important that you highlight this issue. You must obtain a full adult psychological report and forward this with your application. If you have not been tested for dyslexia, but feel you may be dyslexic, then try visiting the British Dyslexia Association at **www.bdadyslexia.org.uk**. An individual who is dyslexic will be provided with the appropriate support depending on their individual needs.

'I tend to procrastinate; what can I do to stop it?'

If you have something to do, do it as soon as you are able. The bigger the task, the higher up your list of things to do it should go. You have a choice – you can either sit in front of your TV feeling that there is a big list of things to do or you can sit in front of the same TV, a little later on, in the knowledge that they have all been done. The latter is probably a preferable place to be. Preparing for the assessment centre is a bit like making a fundamental change to the way in which you live your life; suddenly you have to switch your brain on.

'How do I switch my brain on?'

It is more a state of mind than anything else. If you don't know something, you can find out; if you need to remember something, you can record it; if you can't find something, don't give up until it is found. You approach things in a positive light and aim to push yourself just a bit harder each day. If you forget something, you learn it again and so on.

'I always feel that I am the one who is going to fail; what can I do?'

Try this: listen to those around you and hear just how often they are negative about other people and things; you will be amazed. Listen to yourself and you may be just as surprised to hear yourself doing the same. Now think about your opinion of yourself. Is it negative; do you give yourself a hard time? The answer for many is a resounding 'yes'. For as long as you put yourself down, there you are likely to stay. A positive self-regard (without entering the realms of pure fantasy) is the key to success. So don't beat yourself up and start feeling good about yourself.

The ten top tips for completing your written exercises

1. Plan your work, but not for too long. Take no more time than is absolutely necessary.

2. If you don't know how to spell a word, don't use it.

3. Don't use big words to impress; they are not very impressive when they are spelt incorrectly.

4. Identify your aim.

5. If you know your spelling is not very good, don't just sit there, do something about it!

6. There are words that are often misspelt, so get to know them and learn the correct spellings.

7. Employ your resources wisely; use words that are provided on the instruction sheet.

8. Cross your 't's and dot your 'i's.

9. If you think you are not going to complete the task, don't panic. It is more important to present 'less' correctly than 'more' incorrectly.

10. Check your work!

Part 2 of this book will now offer a number of written exercises. These comprise two parts: the information for the candidate and texts from various sources. They are designed to be similar to the exercises found within the assessment centre.

Part 3 offers specimen responses to those exercises.

References

Cox, P. (2007) *Passing the Police Recruit Assessment Process*. Exeter: Learning Matters.

dictionary.com (2008) Available online at http://dictionary.reference.com (accessed 22 October 2008).

Helprin, M. (1983) *Winter's Tale*. London: Harcourt Brace and Company.

Hickey, J. (2008) *Literacy for QTLS: Achieving the minimum core*. London: Pearson.

The Interview Success Company Ltd (2009) ICED mnemonic, course material. Available online at www.theinterviewsuccesscompany.co.uk (accessed 6 November 2008).

Madsen, S. (2007) *Practical Policing Skills for Student Officers* (2nd edn). Exeter: Learning Matters.

Malthouse, R., Kennard, P. and Roffey-Barentsen, J. (2009) *Interactive Exercises for the Police Recruit Assessment Process: Succeeding at role plays*. Exeter: Learning Matters.

National Policing Improvement Agency (2007) *Welcome Pack*. London: Home Office.

Roffey-Barentsen, J. and Malthouse, R. (2009) *Reflective Practice in the Lifelong Learning Sector*. Exeter: Learning Matters.

SWG Community Blog (2008) Available online at: http://community.spyka.co.uk/showthread.php?t=19921&page=4 (accessed 6 November 2008).

Tolkien, J.R.R. (1988) *The Return of the King. Being the third part of The Lord of the Rings*. London: Unwin.

Further reading

Cox, P. (2007) *Passing the Police Recruit Assessment Process*. Exeter: Learning Matters.

Hickey, J. (2008) *Literacy for QTLS: Achieving the minimum core*. London: Pearson Education.

Malthouse, R., Kennard, P. and Roffey-Barentsen, J. (2009) *Interactive Exercises for the Police Recruit Assessment Process: Succeeding at role plays*. Exeter: Learning Matters.

Useful websites

www.learningmatters.co.uk Offers various police- and law-related publications.

www.theinterviewsuccesscompany.co.uk Offers guidance in relation to passing the assessment centre process and further training.

Part 2
Written exercises

This part of the book offers ten written exercises for you to practise. You have a maximum of 20 minutes per exercise. We recommend that you adhere to this allotted time as this will give you the experience of working under pressure. Further, it will enable you to judge how much of your time to allocate to the reading, planning and completion of the task. It is recommended that you save a little time to check over your work.

Once you have completed each exercise, you can compare the structure of your writing with the specimen answer. It may be that your account differs from the specimen, but this is only to be expected as your own interpretation and the way in which you express yourself in writing are individual. Further, it is unlikely that you will produce an example of the same word count as the specimens presented. This is because the examples have been designed to consider as many aspects of the problems as possible.

We recommend that, if you feel that your writing needs to be improved, you ask a person you feel is suitably experienced to evaluate your work critically. If there is no one you feel you can ask, type your account into a Word document and take note of any grammatical errors or spelling mistakes the computer program identifies. At this stage, be sure to reflect on the mistakes you make, as this will give you a better chance to improve.

Remember, if you always do what you have always done, you will always get what you have always got.

WRITTEN EXERCISE 1

Parking in Central Parade

Candidate information

In this exercise there are four pages of information.

1. Memorandum from Ron Moody, Customer Service Manager, Area HQ.
2. Article from the *Eastshire Times*.
3. Results from recent research project.
4. Letter from Douglas Chipperfield.

You are to provide a written response (a blank form is provided for you to copy and use as a template on which to place your answer).

Candidate information 1.1

Memorandum

To: Customer Service Officer, Eastshire Branch
From: Customer Service Manager, Area HQ
Date: Yesterday
Subject: Parking in Central Parade

Dear Colleague,

Please find attached documents related to the proposal for reducing the amount of time our customers will be able to park in this area. We are concerned primarily with the welfare and safety of our customers. I am sorry I can't assist you any further, but I have a short trip to New York planned with my wife.

Please read and compare the various sources and write a report outlining any issues and potential solutions you feel are appropriate. We have written to the borough council, but as yet we have had no reply.

Do what you can.

Ron Moody

Ron Moody

Customer Service Manager, Area HQ

Candidate information 1.2

Eastshire Times

Restrictions 'a money making scheme'

By Kiri Nunn

Traders in the Eastshire Shopping Centre say they will be facing closure if a waiting restriction planned for the shopping centre's Central Parade goes ahead.

Eastshire Borough Council plans to allow only 20-minute parking on both sides of Parade Street, with no return within the hour, but the news has devastated shopkeepers, who have organised a petition and written letters protesting about the move.

Bonnie Hall, who has run the Alternative Hairdressing Salon for five years, said: 'It will be the end of us. How anyone is expected to get their hair done in 20 minutes is beyond me.

I took over from my Mum full time last year. During that time the council has raised my rent by 60 per cent. With the increased cost of food and utilities, the last thing I need is a restriction on parking.

I have 27 clients who have to be here for two hours. Even an hour is not enough for most of them.'

She went on to say: 'I have a lot of disabled people here and it takes longer than 20 minutes to look after them. If this proposal comes in people will look elsewhere. Keep the two-hour rule – it's worked well for years.' Georgina Speed, who lives nearby, said: 'I have lived here for nearly 21 years and this proposal will not help me park my car any more easily. It just seems to be annoying the local businesses. What they are proposing is simply ridiculous.'

Kim Pierce, the owner of Eastshire Fine Arts, said: 'What the council seems to forget is that the majority of those parking here are elderly, and they simply need more time to do what they need to do.'

Eastshire Lib Dem Cllr Sunil Patel said: 'Businesses here are struggling already. There are residential streets around and people are not going to be happy if customers park in their road.' A borough council spokeswoman said the parking restriction in Central Parade would allow customers to make brief stops at shops and this would be good for businesses because it increases the turnover of potential customers.

Candidate information 1.3

Eastshire Shopping Centre Research Unit

Data: Average per hour use of the parking in Central Parade.

Collated over a three-month period – March to May.

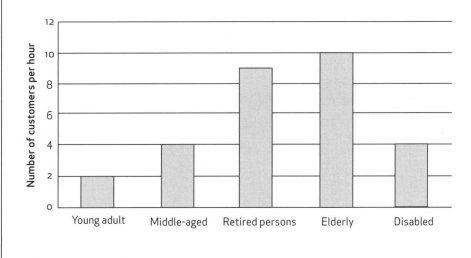

Key:

Young adult	17–34
Middle-aged	35–64
Retired persons	65–79
Elderly	80 plus
Disabled	Indicated by the Blue Badge parking scheme

41

Candidate information 1.4

Letter from Douglas Chipperfield

Dear Mr Moody,

I am writing to you to draw your attention to the fact that the council intends reducing the amount of time I can park my car in Central Parade. I couldn't believe my ears when I heard that they want to reduce our parking time from 2 hours to 20 minutes!

I am disabled, and it takes me about 10 minutes to get out of the car and into the centre. At this rate, by the time I get in, it will be time to turn around and get back to my car; I will have no time to do my shopping.

I don't know what's got into them at the council, only it will not do at all. Please can you take a stand on this for us? I know you understand the needs of all your community, not just the young and the fit.

Please let me know what you are proposing to do on our behalf.

Yours sincerely,

Douglas Chipperfield

Douglas Chipperfield

WRITTEN EXERCISE 1

Report

From: Candidate, Customer Service
To: Ron Moody, Customer Service Manager, Area HQ
Date: Today
Subject: Parking in Central Parade

WRITTEN EXERCISE 2

The removal of the Hayway playground

Candidate information

In this exercise there are four pages of information.

1. Memorandum from Ron Moody, Customer Service Manager, Area HQ.
2. Article from the *Eastshire Times*.
3. Letter from Sam Denton.
4. Results from recent research project.

You are to provide a written response (a blank form is provided on which to place your answer).

Candidate information 2.1

Memorandum

To: Customer Service Officer, Eastshire Branch
From: Customer Service Manager, Area HQ
Date: Yesterday
Subject: The removal of the Hayway playground

Dear Colleague,

Please find attached documents related to the proposal for the temporary removal of the Hayway playground and childminding facilities. There are concerns that the services used by many parents will be lost if the council's plans get the go-ahead. I am sorry I can't assist you any further, but I have to make a long-awaited golf trip to the south of France.

Please read and compare the various sources and write a report outlining any issues and potential solutions you feel are appropriate. We have written to the borough council, but as yet we have had no reply. Please do what you can with the material you have available.

Ron Moody

Ron Moody

Customer Service Manager, Area HQ

Candidate information 2.2

Council to close playground

By Holly Bright

Eastshire Borough Council says the Hayway Playground and childminding facilities will be replaced once work on a flood alleviation scheme has been completed. The playground and facilities, at the rear of the Eastshire Shopping Centre, are used by many children while their parents do the shopping. It is fully supervised by dedicated staff and benefits from a regular patrol from the Eastshire Security Guards.

The Eastshire Times reported last week that the site was earmarked by the council for the flood basin.

David Ward, Cultural and Community Development Manager, confirmed that the council had looked into the possibility of relocating the play areas, but has been unable to find a suitable alternative site.

Following a previous article in this paper, a council spokesman said in response: 'It is not the intention of the council to take away this play facility from this area of the borough. However, the playground is within an area that will be affected by flood alleviation works in association with the Eastshire Valley Scheme. This means that, at some stage, the site on which the play facility currently stands will need to be excavated to form a basin that could collect rainwater in the event of a severe flood. It is the council's intention either to put an improved facility back on the site once the works are completed, or to find a new location nearby that meets the needs of residents. The new play area will be designed following consultation with local people. In the meantime, the council intends to carry out minor improvement works to ensure that the site remains safe and enjoyable for local children to use.'

However, the Eastshire Times can reveal exclusively from an inside source that the council has no intention of putting an improved facility back on the site!

Candidate information 2.3

Letter from Sam Denton

Dear Mr Moody,

I would like to draw your attention to the fact that the Eastshire Borough Council is planning to get rid of the children's play area and childminding facilities in Hayway. This will affect me and my family in two ways. First, a stream runs past the play area. It is cordoned off and offers no danger to the children. A wooden bridge enables me to walk over the stream and into the shopping centre. Second, I rely on the scheme they have at the playground. They have a system where they look after our children while we do the shopping and such like and it costs next to nothing.

If they get rid of the bridge when the flood regulator comes in, which I heard they will, then I will have to walk an extra mile and a half to get to the centre, so I may as well use the local shops as it will be quicker. If they get rid of the Hayway playground, I definitely won't be able to shop there any more. It's not easy with five children at the best of times.

Yours sincerely,

Sam Denton

Sam Denton

Candidate information 2.4

Eastshire Shopping Centre Research Unit

Data: Attendance of children aged between 3 and 12 at the Hayway childminding facility

Average figures collated over one year

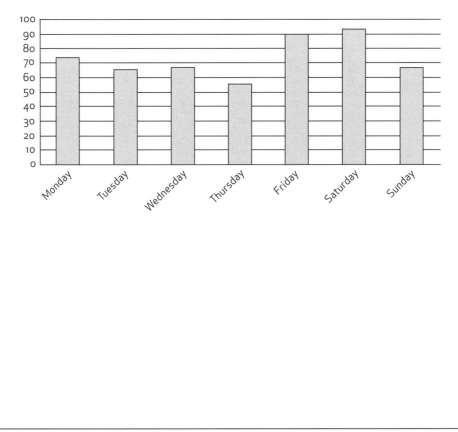

WRITTEN EXERCISE 2

Report

From: Candidate, Customer Service
To: Ron Moody, Customer Service Manager, Area HQ
Date: Today
Subject: The removal of the Hayway playground

_____
_____
_____
_____
_____
_____
_____
_____
_____
_____
_____
_____
_____
_____
_____
_____
_____
_____
_____
_____
_____
_____
_____
_____
_____
_____
_____
_____
_____
_____
_____
_____
_____
_____
_____
_____

WRITTEN EXERCISE 3

The parking situation at the Muslim Education Centre

Candidate information

In this exercise there are four pages of information.

1. Memorandum from Ron Moody, Customer Service Manager, Area HQ.
2. Article from the *Eastshire Times*.
3. Letter from Roger McMillan.
4. Results from recent research project.

You are to provide a written response (a blank form is provided on which to place your answer).

Candidate information 3.1

Memorandum

To: Customer Service Officer, Eastshire Branch
From: Customer Service Manager, Area HQ
Date: Yesterday
Subject: The parking situation at the Muslim Education Centre

Dear Colleague,

Please find attached documents related to the proposal for the difficulty the Muslim Education Centre is experiencing with the parking situation. I am sorry I can't assist you any further, but I will be skiing in Italy for the next couple of weeks.

Please read and compare the various sources and write a report outlining any issues and potential solutions you feel are appropriate. We have written to the borough council, but as yet we have had no reply. Do what you can.

Ron Moody

Ron Moody

Customer Service Manager, Area HQ

Candidate information 3.2

Eastshire Times

Parking mayhem at Muslim centre

By Kiri Nunn

As the parking situation at the Eastshire Muslim Education Centre deteriorates, the local residents have vowed to fight a decision to build a morgue within the building. The plans received the go-ahead at a recent planning committee meeting. It is proposed that a building containing a cold room for the storage of bodies prior to burial will be built at the Eastshire Muslim Education Centre, All Hallows – the former Church of England church. The plans were put forward by Mr Rashid, from the Eastshire Islamic Trust, who uses the centre. We can reveal that the council received 89 letters of objection, one petition signed by 21 people and a noise diary. More than 24 residents were present at the meeting, a number of them clutching placards saying 'Eastshire getting stuffed by the council'.

Mr Osborn, a spokesman for Mr Rashid, said: 'I feel the local residents are being vindictive. Why would they wish us not to have a morgue? We always ask our users to make as little noise as possible. The main concern was parking and we have taken this very seriously and intend to expand it. During the last two years two people have died while at the mosque. The morgue is not a commercial business. It will only be used for a short time while the bodies are washed and then kept in the cold room for a few hours.' Cllr Elizabeth Wall said: 'For all the years I have been a councillor I can never remember such a reaction to an application.' After the meeting Alan Sinclair, a local resident, said: 'The council agrees that our quality of life will be affected, but this doesn't

matter. We will have been left at the mercy of the Eastshire Islamic Trust, which we feel has no respect for us. We will fight it and be extra vigilant of what's going on at the site. If they approve plans to extend the car park it will send out a message that we are just not important.'

Michael Rowan, from the nearby Tennis and Bowls Club, said: 'I don't know what the fuss is all about. We are five minutes' walk away from the Muslim centre and have nearly 250 car parking spaces. The Muslim people are more than welcome to park there whenever they wish. We would be pleased to allocate some spaces, only no one has approached us. They seem more intent on demonstrating about morgues.'

Candidate information 3.3

Letter from Roger McMillan

Dear Mr Moody,

As you know, I am a local business person and I represent the Eastshire Business Organisation. I am writing to you about the parking at the shopping centre. My customers and others are unable to park their cars in the centre car park due to the worshippers at the local mosque going to pray.

Eastshire Borough Council's aim, we are told, is to enhance the quality of life for Eastshire residents. We feel very strongly that the council's handling of this case is a direct contradiction of this statement. When the Eastshire Islamic Trust took ownership of the building, we were told in writing by Mr Rashid that the site was an educational centre. On the same document he also assured us that it was not their intention to convert the site into a mosque. Now there are large numbers of worshippers coming to prayers five times a day. We have counted 190 people arriving at the site and 350 people for Friday prayers.

They do have a car park, but there are only enough places for 50 cars. The mosque is situated just outside the shopping centre but is having a knock-on effect. Please can you use your considerable influence to do something about this please?

Yours sincerely.

Roger McMillan

Roger McMillan

Candidate information 3.4

Eastshire Shopping Centre Research Unit

Data: Prayer times and parking at the East Side car park

Data exist indicating a direct correlation between Muslim prayer times and the car park being full to maximum capacity. The problem is compounded by the prayer times changing each day:

> *Muslims observe five formal prayers each day. The timings of these prayers are spaced fairly evenly throughout the day, so that one is constantly reminded of God and given opportunities to seek His guidance and forgiveness. In modern times, daily prayer schedules are often printed which precisely pinpoint the beginning of each prayer time.*

		October	May
Fajr	Offered between the beginning of dawn and sunrise	04.57	03.00
Dhuhr	Offered after the declining of the sun	11.44	12.57
Asr	Offered before sunset	14.08	17.01
Mayhrib	Offered after sunset	16.36	20.24
Isha	Offered after the disappearance of the twilight	18.22	22.43

The prayers take place before dawn, at noon, in the afternoon, at sunset and in the evening. A comparison is offered between prayer times in October and six months later in May.

(From: http://islam.about.com/bl_prayertimes.htm (accessed 30 October 2008))

WRITTEN EXERCISE 3

Report

From: Candidate, Customer Service
To: Ron Moody, Customer Service Manager, Area HQ
Date: Today
Subject: The parking situation at the Muslim Education Centre

WRITTEN EXERCISE 4

Expanding the drink limit zone

Candidate information

In this exercise there are four pages of information.

1. Memorandum from Ron Moody, Customer Service Manager, Area HQ.
2. Article from the *Eastshire Times*.
3. Article from the Eastshire Borough Council website.
4. Letter from Rosano Romualdez and Carlos Fracisco.

You are to provide a written response (a blank form is provided on which to place your answer).

Candidate information 4.1

Memorandum

To: Customer Service Officer, Eastshire Branch
From: Customer Service Manager, Area HQ
Date: Yesterday
Subject: Expanding the drink limit zone

Dear Colleague,

Please find attached documents related to the proposal to extend what is referred to as the 'cumulative impact zone' in this area. The proposals are causing a bit of a stir, as you will see in the information contained in the attached reports. I am sorry I can't assist you any further, but I am taking a much-needed break in Egypt.

Please read and compare the various sources and write a report outlining any issues and potential solutions you feel are appropriate. We have not had the opportunity to contact the borough council, but have provided information from their website.

Ron Moody

Ron Moody

Customer Service Manager, Area HQ

Candidate information 4.2

Eastshire Times

Drink limit zone may expand

By Holly Bright

Consultation is due to begin on the expansion of a zone introduced to limit the number of licensed premises in the town.

Eastshire Borough Council's executive has agreed that officers can start consultation with authorities and interested parties about expanding the current 'cumulative impact zone' as part of the alcohol saturation policy. The new policy will have the effect of restricting the number of licensed premises in an area where crime and disorder are an issue. It will focus on premises that are located in known trouble spots. This means that, if you apply for a licence in one of these areas, it is highly unlikely that it will be granted.

Extensions of the zone would see the Eastshire Shopping Centre being included.

A report carried out by council officials said that the effect of the policy is to 'create an alcohol-free zone unless the applicant can demonstrate that they will not add to the area's issues or impact on one or more of their objectives'. John Sheppard, the local Lib Dem councillor, suggested when questioned: 'There is nothing for the average 9 to 5 business to concern themselves with. The problems this initiative deals with are those that typically occur at closing time on Friday and Saturday nights.' The findings of the report are due to be presented to the executive of the council later this month.

Candidate information 4.3

Article from the Eastshire Borough Council website

The Licensing Act 2003 received Royal Assent on 10 July 2003 and came into effect on 24 November 2005.

The new Act introduces the following changes to licensing laws in England and Wales:

- flexible opening hours, with the potential for up to 24-hour opening, seven days a week, subject to consideration of the impact on local residents;

- a single licence for a premises or a club that provides 'licensable activities'; this includes: the retail sale of alcohol; the supply of alcohol by or on behalf of a club to a member or guest; the provision of regulated entertainment;

- a system of personal licences that allows holders to sell or serve alcohol for consumption on or off any premises possessing a premises licence;

- the issuing/granting of licences for all licensable activities to be the responsibility of local councils.

The Act has four principal 'licensing objectives':

- prevention of crime and disorder;

- prevention of public nuisance;

- promotion to public safety;

- protection of children from harm.

Eastshire Borough Council's Licensing Policy has been written based on these objectives and forms the basis for considering licence applications.

Candidate information 4.4

Letter from Rosano Romualdez and Carlos Fracisco

Dear Mr Moody,

We are writing to draw your attention to the fact that the council intends expanding what they call the 'cumulative impact zone'. The difficulty we face is that our premises, Roscarlos, have recently applied for a licence to sell alcohol for consumption off the premises. We open at 9 a.m. and close at 6 p.m., Monday to Saturday. We sell goods that are typical of a small supermarket. The licence we have applied for would enable us to sell alcohol only to be consumed off the premises.

We read in the paper that the council's policy will mean that an application for a premises license such as ours will be refused unless we can demonstrate that we will not add to the area's issues or impact on one or more of their objectives.

Our problem is that I know there is an issue with crime and disorder on Friday and Saturday nights on occasion within the shopping centre. We have witnessed drunken behaviour as the pubs close. But is that any reason to prevent decent law-abiding citizens from setting up a business? This has gone too far; is there no end to this? Does this mean that, if someone is found shoplifting in one of the shops, it will be closed down? We feel the law is being used indiscriminately. Please tell us what you intend doing about it.

Yours sincerely,

Rosano Romualdez

Carlos Fracisco

Rosano Romualdez and Carlos Fracisco

WRITTEN EXERCISE 4

Report

From: Candidate, Customer Service
To: Ron Moody, Customer Service Manager, Area HQ
Date: Today
Subject: Expanding the drink limit zone

WRITTEN EXERCISE 5

The closure of 200 spaces at the Eastshire Shopping Centre car park

Candidate information

In this exercise there are four pages of information.

1. Memorandum from Ron Moody, Customer Service Manager, Area HQ.
2. Article from the *Eastshire Times*.
3. E-mail from Wenda Gooderham.
4. List of available parking during the renovation at the Eastshire Shopping Centre car park.

You are to provide a written response (a blank form is provided on which to place your answer).

Candidate information 5.1

Memorandum

To:	Customer Service Officer, Eastshire Branch
From:	Customer Service Manager, Area HQ
Date:	Yesterday
Subject:	Closure of 200 spaces at the Eastshire Shopping Centre car park

Dear Colleague,

Please find attached documents related to the proposal to resurface the Eastshire Shopping Centre car park. The proposals are having a knock-on effect, as you will notice from the attached letter and newspaper cutting, etc. I am sorry I can't assist you any further, but I have a cruise booked in the Caribbean for the next couple of weeks.

Please read and compare the various sources and write a report outlining any issues and potential solutions you feel are appropriate.

Ron Moody

Ron Moody

Customer Service Manager, Area HQ

Candidate information 5.2

Parking suspended: 200 spaces axed

By Kiri Nunn

The Eastshire Times learned of proposals to axe 200 parking spaces at the Eastshire Shopping Centre (ESC) to make room for resurfacing work. In two months' time the first and second floors of the ESC multi-storey car park are to be resurfaced, causing possible mayhem and a parking nightmare. Only the top floor of three will remain serviceable. This will mean that parking will be reduced from 300 spaces to a mere 120 spaces. The work will take five days to complete.

As a result, many shoppers will have to make other arrangements to park their cars over the period. Tempers are already rising as a result of the news. When asked about the closure, Cynthia Cockroft said: 'This is typical of the level of consultation we have become used to over the years. Nobody has bothered to tell us a thing about the closures.' Gerald Cockroft added: 'This is going to impact upon our business hugely. Our customers use the multi-storey car park as it is convenient if they are carrying the goods

they have purchased. Now what are they going to do? The nearest alternative car park is at the railway station and you could not describe that as being close.' Ajay Mandalia from the Eastshire Borough Council said: 'This work represents essential maintenance. If we do not resurface the floors now, the uneven surface may be the cause of an injury. People expect to be able to push trolleys over this surface, but the way it is at present is potentially a health and safety issue.'

Candidate information 5.3

E-mail from Wenda Gooderham

From: wenda@leisurecentre.ds.uk
To: ronaldtarquinmoody@eastshirecentre.ds.uk
Date: Yesterday
Subject: The closure of 200 spaces at the Eastshire Shopping Centre car park

Dear Mr Moody,

As you know, I am the manager of the Eastshire Leisure Centre, and I am a bit concerned that my gym members won't be able to park when visiting the leisure centre during your car park improvements. Twenty of my customers pay £55 per month for gold membership and won't be too impressed to arrive at the gym to find shoppers parked in their reserved spaces.

As you know, our members get a 10 per cent discount at the Cockroft sports shop in your shopping centre. This brings in a lot of trade for you at the centre. If you go ahead with your plans to use our car park spaces, I will consider withdrawing our special agreement.

Wenda Gooderham

Candidate information 5.4

Available parking during the renovation at the Eastshire Shopping Centre car park

Eastshire Shopping Centre car park

Open 0600–2200: 1 minute from the shopping centre

Only 120 spaces remaining on the top floor during renovations

- 20 spaces are reserved for gold membership pass holders attending the Eastshire Leisure Centre

- 80 spaces are remaining at £1 pay and display for 1 hour

- 10 for disabled users

- 10 for parents/guardians accompanied by children

Owned by Eastshire Borough Council

Railway Station car park

Open 24 hours: 5 minutes walk from the shopping centre

350 spaces of which only 200 are used by travellers

Pay and display £2.50 per day

Owned by East2West Trains

Eastshire High Street and East Hill Road car parks

High St.: 80 metered spaces at £1 per hour

East Hill Road: Unrestricted parking for 60 cars

Both are about 15–20 minutes from the shopping centre

WRITTEN EXERCISE 5

Report

From: Candidate, Customer Service
To: Ron Moody, Customer Service Manager, Area HQ
Date: Today
Subject: The closure of 200 spaces at the Eastshire Shopping Centre car park

_____

_____

_____

_____

_____

_____

_____

_____

_____

_____

_____

_____

_____

_____

_____

_____

_____

_____

_____

_____

_____

_____

_____

_____

_____

_____

_____

_____

_____

_____

_____

_____

_____

WRITTEN EXERCISE 6

Season ticket protest

Candidate information

In this exercise there are five pages of information.

1. Memorandum from Ron Moody, Customer Service Manager, Area HQ.
2. Article from the *Eastshire Times*.
3. E-mail from Misha Yakovleva.
4. List of available parking during the renovation at the Eastshire Shopping Centre car park.
5. E-mail from Sgt Mark Thompson.

You are to provide a written response (a blank form is provided on which to place your answer).

Candidate information 6.1

Memorandum

To: Customer Service Officer, Eastshire Branch
From: Customer Service Manager, Area HQ
Date: Yesterday
Subject: Season ticket protest

Dear Colleague,

Please find attached documents related to the proposal to resurface the Eastshire Shopping Centre car park. It appears that this issue is not over just yet. The proposals are having a knock-on effect, as you will notice from the attached letter and newspaper cutting, etc. I am sorry I can't assist you any further, but I am having a well-earned, but short, break in Lapland.

Please read and compare the various sources and write a report outlining any issues and potential solutions you feel are appropriate.

Ron Moody

Ron Moody

Customer Service Manager, Area HQ

Candidate information 6.2

Eastshire Times

Season ticket protest

By Holly Bright

A short while ago, the Eastshire Times brought to you details of proposals to axe 200 parking spaces at the Eastshire Shopping Centre (ESC) to make room for resurfacing work.

This work has been delayed due to the fact that serious cracks were found in the floor once the old surface had been removed. As a result, it is unlikely that the two floors in the car park will be open to the public within the next two months. Tracy Bell from the council explained: 'Apparently the weight of some of the larger vehicles has damaged the floor. When this building was built the architects had not envisaged that the modern 4x4 vehicles would be parking in the car park. Times change and now the Chelsea tractors are every-where it seems.'

In their wisdom, the powers that be have decided to make use of the nearby railway station car park. This has infuriated some people who are now unable to park their cars in the car park due to the shoppers' cars. To make things worse, other people wishing to use the car park to shop are unable to gain access as they often find it totally full. Georgina Speed said: 'The situation is beyond a joke. No one is happy that the car park is just too full all the time.' Martin Reed, a regular commuter, added: 'I have been commuting for nearly 30 years. The one thing you don't expect to find is that there are no places available whatso-ever. I pay a considerable amount of money for a season ticket; this includes a token to park. Obviously it was a waste of money. The other day I had no choice but to go back home and ask my wife to drop me back off. Without her I don't know what I would have done. It's too far to walk, you see. I will be asking for my money back from the railway company.'

Mr Reed is not alone; we spoke to a number of angry season ticket holders, many of whom shared the same feel-ings of exasperation and disbelief that the authorities have managed to get it so badly wrong.

Candidate information 6.3

E-mail from Misha Yakovleva

From: mishayakovleva@yahoohoo.com
To: ronaldtarquinmoody@eastshirecentre.ds.uk
Date: Yesterday
Subject: Parking for season ticket holders

Dear Mr Moody,

I am contacting you to complain about the fact that you have decided to redirect the cars from the Eastshire Shopping Centre car park to the Railway Station car park. I am a season ticket holder and should be able to park my car to get to work. I can't because it is completely full whenever I want to use it. Even early in the morning it is full of the cars of people who I know work in the shopping centre. This cannot be right.

I now have put my car in the East Hill Road car park, but I face a long walk to the station. The other day I had the side of my car scraped from one end to the next right down to the metal. Surely you can provide some protection for me? What about CCTV or extra security guards? What about reimbursing me for my wasted parking expenses at the station?

You are responsible for this mess, so please sort it out.

Misha Yakovleva

Candidate information 6.4

Available parking during the renovation at the Eastshire Shopping Centre car park

Eastshire Shopping Centre car park

Open 0600–2200: 1 minute from the shopping centre

Only 120 spaces remaining on the top floor during renovations

- 20 spaces are reserved for gold membership pass holders attending the Eastshire Leisure Centre

- 80 spaces are remaining at £1 pay and display for 1 hour

- 10 for disabled users

- 10 for parents/guardians accompanied by children

Owned by Eastshire Borough Council

Railway Station car park

Open 24 hours: 5 minutes walk from the shopping centre

350 spaces of which only 200 are used by travellers

Pay and display £2.50 per day

Owned by East2West Trains

Eastshire High Street and East Hill Road car parks

High St.: 80 metered spaces at £1 per hour

East Hill Road: Unrestricted parking for 60 cars

Both are about 15–20 minutes from the shopping centre

Candidate information 6.5

E-mail from Sgt Mark Thompson

From: markthompson@eastshirepolice.uk
To: ronaldtarquinmoody@eastshirecentre.ds.uk
Date: Yesterday
Subject: The potential increase in vehicle-related crime

Dear Mr Moody,

I am the Police Sergeant for the Eastshire Safer Neighbourhood team. I have just seen an article on the Eastshire Times website relating to the extended closure of the car park in the shopping centre. I have checked our records and I see that a similar situation happened two years ago when your top floor was resurfaced. I wish to point out that vehicle crime went through the roof for that week. Two cars were stolen, 12 had their windows smashed and 14 tyres were slashed.

While the police won't apply for any temporary parking restriction during this time, I feel that, if you direct your customers to park in Eastshire High Street and East Hill Road, you will be directly adding to the opportunity for crime. This is a shame because we have done so much good work together previously to drive crime down. Please note that I cannot supply any extra patrolling officers due to sickness and annual leave.

Mark Thompson

Sergeant, Eastshire police

WRITTEN EXERCISE 6

Report

From: Candidate, Customer Service
To: Ron Moody, Customer Service Manager, Area HQ
Date: Today
Subject: Season ticket protest

_____

_____

_____

_____

_____

_____

_____

_____

_____

_____

_____

_____

_____

_____

_____

_____

_____

_____

_____

_____

_____

_____

_____

_____

_____

_____

_____

_____

_____

_____

_____

_____

_____

_____

_____

WRITTEN EXERCISE 7

The increase in road traffic collisions

Candidate information

In this exercise there are four pages of information.

1. Memorandum from Ron Moody, Customer Service Manager, Area HQ.
2. Article from the *Eastshire Times*.
3. Data relating to accidents in Railway Approach.
4. E-mail from Gary Ayton, Road Watch.

You are to provide a written response (a blank form is provided on which to place your answer).

75

Candidate information 7.1

Memorandum

To: Customer Service Officer, Eastshire Branch
From: Customer Service Manager, Area HQ
Date: Yesterday
Subject: Increase in road traffic collisions

Dear Colleague,

Please find attached documents related to the increase in road traffic accidents outside the Railway Station car park. Apparently, the people using the car park make their way over the road towards the shopping centre, rather than to the railway station. I have checked the jurisdiction and it falls within our area, so we are responsible for doing something about it. I think the figures speak for themselves.

I am sorry I can't assist you any further, but I am going into hospital to undergo a small operation. Please read and compare the various sources and write a report outlining any issues and potential solutions you feel are appropriate.

Ron Moody

Ron Moody

Customer Service Manager, Area HQ

Candidate information 7.2

Eastshire Times

Car park carnage
By Kiri Nunn

A short while ago, the Eastshire Times brought to you details of proposals to axe 200 parking spaces at the Eastshire Shopping Centre (ESC) to make room for resurfacing work. We then heard that the car park would not be reopening for some considerable time because of the repairs that were needed to the car park floor. The shoppers were advised to use the Railway Station car park and many did so, unaware of the dangers they were to face.

Accidents have risen to an astounding level in Railway Approach, outside the Railway Station car park; the speed limit there is 40 mph. A police spokesperson said: 'The problem is that the car park is designed for people using the railway station, so there is nothing to assist people to cross the road.

There was an old-style zebra crossing, but the council decided to get rid of it the last time the road was resurfaced. As a result, pedestrians are being put in a position of danger as they attempt to cross the road. We would urge people to find a suitable place to cross, not just one that presents the shortest route.'

When questioned about the removal of the zebra crossing, Tracy Bell from the council said: 'At the time, research was undertaken to identify if it was economically feasible to replace the crossing with a more up-to-date pedestrian crossing. Our research indicated that very few pedestrians crossed the road at that point. It appeared that nearly 99.9 per cent of those using the station used bicycles, drove or were given a lift. As a result, it was decided that

there was no need to replace any form of pedestrian crossing at that point. There was no way that we could have anticipated this situation.'

Sally Parr, a local shopper, said: 'This is appalling, I cannot believe that people have been advised to park here to attend the shopping centre when clearly there is no infrastructure to ensure their safety. Surely those in charge could have anticipated the problems we are experiencing. The traffic moves too quickly along this stretch of the road. People find it very difficult to estimate the speed of traffic. I am not surprised people are getting hurt. It will only be a matter of time before someone is killed. Something must be done immediately.'

Candidate information 7.3

Eastshire Shopping Centre Research Unit

Data: Collisions in Railway Approach

The figures from August to December represent the situation before the extended use of the Railway Station car park by shoppers. The figures indicate a sharp increase in road collisions from December to February. March is included but only data for the first two weeks are available at present.

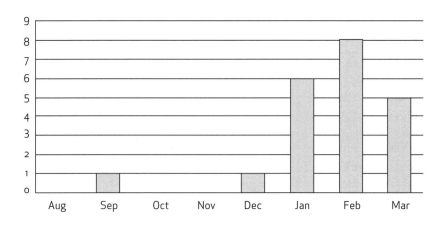

Candidate information 7.4

E-mail from Gary Ayton, Road Watch

From: garyayton@roadwatch.gov.hr.uk
To: ronaldtarquinmoody@eastshirecentre.ds.uk
Date: Yesterday
Subject: The increase in motor vehicle collisions

Dear Mr Moody,

I am a member of Road Watch, a local government organisation set up to identify significant issues in relation to the use of our roads. I have just seen the figures for accidents within your jurisdiction. I notice that they are worryingly high for the second month, indicating a distinct increase in road casualties. I feel that we must act as soon as possible as it is obvious that this situation is intolerable. We can offer you advice in relation to your options at this stage. There is no time for lengthy meetings with the various interested parties; someone could die if you do not act quickly and positively.

I have spoken to Sgt Mark Thompson in relation to this matter. Unfortunately, he is unable to supply any extra patrolling officers due to sickness and annual leave.

A word of caution – whatever you do, you must ensure that it will not have an adverse effect on the surrounding traffic; we don't want gridlock elsewhere.

Gary Ayton

Road Watch

WRITTEN EXERCISE 7

Report

From: Candidate, Customer Service
To: Ron Moody, Customer Service Manager, Area HQ
Date: Today
Subject: The increase in road traffic collisions

_____
_____
_____
_____
_____
_____
_____
_____
_____
_____
_____
_____
_____
_____
_____
_____
_____
_____
_____
_____
_____
_____
_____
_____
_____
_____
_____
_____
_____
_____

WRITTEN EXERCISE 8

The wearing of hoodies

Candidate information

In this exercise there are four pages of information.

1. Memorandum from Ron Moody, Customer Service Manager, Area HQ.
2. Article from the *Eastshire Times*.
3. Letter from Keith Giannoni.
4. E-mail from Chrissie Coles.

You are to provide a written response (a blank form is provided on which to place your answer).

Candidate information 8.1

Memorandum

To: Customer Service Officer, Eastshire Branch
From: Customer Service Manager, Area HQ
Date: Yesterday
Subject: The wearing of hoodies

Dear Colleague,

Please find attached documents related to the proposed ban on people wearing hoodies within the Eastshire Shopping Centre. This is causing a bit of a kerfuffle. What you must remember is that the council does not have jurisdiction over us – it is only a proposal and we can agree or disagree as we feel fit.

I am sorry I can't assist you any further, but I am going to Switzerland to recover fully from my recent operation. The doctor said it should help relieve the stress of my work.

Please read and compare the various sources and write a report outlining any issues and potential solutions you feel are appropriate.

Ron Moody

Ron Moody

Customer Service Manager, Area HQ

Candidate information 8.2

Eastshire Times

Hoodieya think you are?

By Holly Bright

Shoppers in the Eastshire Centre are up in arms following a proposed ban on hoodies by the local borough council. Under new regulations to be introduced next month, any person found wearing a hoodie will be asked to leave the premises. This has sparked a wave of complaints from shoppers and local businesses alike. Georgina Speed, who lives nearby said: 'All my children wear hoodies; it's what people of their age want. I think it is discriminatory to do this. Has the council not heard of the age discrimination act?'

James Reid, a local retailer from the Boomerang Market, observed: 'I think they are confusing the issue here; you see it is a one-way correlation. Most of the people who are committing crimes are wearing hoodies, but not all the people who wear hoodies are criminals. We get lots of teenagers in my shop, and most of them in fact, except for one or two, are very nice people.'

However, not everyone agrees. Harold Townsend, a pensioner, was recently mugged while on his way home from shopping. We told him about the proposals and he said: 'I agree totally with the ban. Those kids wearing hoodies are a menace. You know they couldn't pick them up on CCTV because no one could see their faces. It's not right; they shouldn't be able to get away with it.'

Police Sergeant Mark Thompson from the Safer Neighbourhood team said: 'It's all about being reasonable. What we must ask ourselves is this – is it a reasonable thing to ask people not to wear hoodies because it makes some people feel uneasy? Yes, the kids have rights, but so does everyone else. If hoodies were not linked to crime, there would be no problem, but the sad fact is, they are.'

The Eastshire Times spoke to a group of young people who were wearing hoodies in the Eastshire Centre, and who wished to remain anonymous. But they suggested: 'This is unfair and racist, right, 'cos, right, you wouldn't get the Muslims to take off their head stuff and that's the same as what we are wearing, well practically.' One of the group later informed me that she had recently been arrested for shoplifting and assaulting a security guard.

Candidate information 8.3

Letter from Keith Giannoni

Dear Mr Moody,

I have just visited your shopping centre and have noticed a number of posters advertising the fact that people wearing hoodies will not be welcome. I find this decision to be ill thought out. As the Manager of the Olympic Body gym, I have provided our 20 gold members with top of the range leisurewear as a thank you for their loyalty to the gym. This includes a hooded sweat top with our logo emblazoned on the chest. Many of those members arrive and leave the gym in their tops.

This new dress code proposal would mean that they will either have to change or avoid using the shopping centre before or after their workout. Needless to say, if you pursue this course of action, I will reconsider whether this shopping centre is a suitable location for my business. Let's face it, your fees are not the cheapest in Eastshire, are they?

Yours sincerely,

KEITH GIANNONI

Keith Giannoni

Candidate information 8.4

E-mail from Chrissie Coles

From: chrissiecoles@gov.social.uk
To: ronaldtarquinmoody@eastshirecentre.ds.uk
Date: Yesterday
Subject: The perception of teenagers, hoodies and crime

Dear Mr Moody,

The following represents research from a local blog in relation to teenagers' perceptions of wearing hoodies. I hope it assists you in the decision-making process.

Chrissie Coles

Topic – The wearing of hoodies

'Well its annoying, and now the media have taken it up who knows where it will go. I don't personally feel intimidated by hoodie-wearing young people – even if they're in a group. I won't allow myself to change my views at all, due to the actions and behaviour of a few chavs. Let's face it, some people who do crime wear hoodies, but they are a minority.'

'It's not necessarily chavs but yeah I agree with you. Unfortunately, that is life. It is usually the minority who spoil things for the majority of people.'

'Right i'm at home now so am wearing a hoody cos it's quite cold, but like if I went out in it, I'd probably end up harassed for covering my head, thats stupid.'

'It's probably a good thing yobs wear something that makes you wary of them in the first place, i mean if you saw someone walking towards you in a balaclava you'd cross the road right? if hoodies didnt wear hoodies then how would you know to avoid them? they'd look like everyone else and thats not good.'

'The main reason why people are intimidated by normal people wearing hooded tops is because of stupidity, like trying to get them banned and news articles referring to them as not thugs, but 'hoodies'.'

(Based on conversations within SWG community.spyka.co.uk)

WRITTEN EXERCISE 8

Report

From: Candidate, Customer Service
To: Ron Moody, Customer Service Manager, Area HQ
Date: Today
Subject: The wearing of hoodies

_____
_____
_____
_____
_____
_____
_____
_____
_____
_____
_____
_____
_____
_____
_____
_____
_____
_____
_____
_____
_____
_____
_____
_____
_____
_____
_____
_____
_____
_____
_____
_____

WRITTEN EXERCISE 9

The theft of metal

Candidate information

In this exercise there are four pages of information.

1. Memorandum from Ron Moody, Customer Service Manager, Area HQ.
2. Article from the *Eastshire Times*.
3. Letter from Lindsey Thornberg, Shop Watch.
4. E-mail from Dominic Gannon, Drugs Watch.

You are to provide a written response (a blank form is provided on which to place your answer).

Candidate information 9.1

Memorandum

To: Customer Service Officer, Eastshire Branch
From: Customer Service Manager, Area HQ
Date: Yesterday
Subject: The theft of metal

Dear Colleague,

Please find attached documents related to the spiralling problem of metal theft. This really is a sign of the times. I am sorry I can't assist you any further, but I am going on Safari in the near future.

Please read and compare the various sources and write a report outlining any issues and potential solutions you feel are appropriate.

Ron Moody

Ron Moody

Customer Service Manager, Area HQ

Candidate information 9.2

Eastshire Times

Money in brass

By Kiri Nunn

Scrap metal thieves are tapping into a wide variety of sources – from church roofs to drain-hole covers in the Eastshire area. The thefts have been sparked by the soaring price of metals around the world. Much of the stolen metal and copper cabling is sold to illegal dealers who sell it off to be shipped abroad.

Now the Safer Eastshire Partnership is asking the public to help stem the theft by supplying information on suspicious behaviour that could lead to arrests. People are being asked to watch out for activities such as dismantling motor vehicles or storing large quantities of industrial cabling on property.

Inspector Dino Gomez of the Eastshire police said: 'We know the theft of all types of scrap metal is up; it is sold to illegal dealers who ship it abroad. In August, the biggest ever seizure of suspected stolen metal, worth over £700,000, was made in Staffordshire and we intend to crack down on anyone caught dealing illegally in scrap metal. However it's not only the dealers we're after. I'd urge members of the community to report any suspicious activity they see.'

Last month, two men, who had been spotted by residents in Eastshire trying to steal hundreds of feet of electricity cable awaiting installation by contractors, were sentenced at Eastshire Crown Court. The Safer Eastshire Partnership, which includes Eastshire Borough Ccouncil, local residents and the Eastshire police, points out that the Scrap Metal Dealers' Act demands that any person or business dealing in scrap metal is registered with the council and that all records must be kept for examination on demand. Cllr Melanie Cook, the council's portfolio holder for community safety, said: 'We're appealing for information and are particularly interested in the back-street dealers. We would encourage anyone with information to contact the police or ourselves.'

Candidate information 9.3

Letter from Lindsey Thornberg, Shop Watch

Dear Mr Moody,

I am contacting you as the representative for the Shop Watch scheme. We have a problem that only became apparent after we realised that what we thought were one-offs were in fact a pattern of behaviour. People are stealing metal, any metal that is not stapled down and some that is. All Hallows Church, now the Eastshire Muslim Education Centre, had the lead and copper from its roof stolen. The problem is that they don't know when it happened exactly as the first they knew about it was when the weather changed for the worse and the leaks became obvious. Mr Rashid says it is going to cost thousands, but he thinks he can claim under the Ecclesiastic Insurance.

Last week, the Eastshire Primary School became a target. Thieves stole the copper roof and it is estimated that it will cost £30,000 in repair bills. The Buddha statue was also taken from outside the temple; this was awful as it was a gift to Eastshire from the people of Tibet in the 1950s.

Small businesses are being hit also; the other day we noticed that the metal grates that run alongside the pavement and act as cover for the drains had been taken. This now represents a health and safety issue. The metal stands used for the market have completely disappeared; when not in use, these have been left folded up in a pile for years without any trouble. We lost power the other day; the reason for this was that someone had tried to steal the copper power lines from the electricity substation; the lines were live. I think they had quite a shock.

We have a problem, so please help us with this challenge.

Yours sincerely,

Lindsey Thornberg

Lindsey Thornberg, Shop Watch

Candidate information 9.4

E-mail from Dominic Gannon, Drugs Watch

From: dominicgannon@drugswatch.gov.uk
To: ronaldtarquinmoody@eastshirecentre.ds.uk
Date: Yesterday
Subject: The perception of theft

Dear Mr Moody,

I have been informed that you are researching the theft of metal. Our own research indicates that frequently the underlying problem is drugs. Increasingly, as the high value of metals such as copper is causing an escalation in the scrap metal trade, drug addicts steal items they can sell to feed their habit.

In extreme cases, they are stealing anything, from air-conditioning units and catalytic converters, to electrical cable, old cars, manhole covers and copper pipes, in fact just about anything that has some value. Most of the crime is being committed at night when there is less chance of being caught. But this type of crime is not restricted to the hours of darkness. The key to prevention is to make your community more aware of what is happening, make them inquisitive and provide them with someone who can assist them in the event of any suspicious behaviour.

For example, this is an emerging crime, so not everyone is aware that it is happening. If they see someone apparently working with metal, they can ask themselves if this seems suspicious: if it does, the appropriate people should be called. Doing nothing will undoubtedly make this situation worse. I hope this assists you.

Dominic Gannon

Drugs Watch

WRITTEN EXERCISE 9

Report

From: Candidate, Customer Service
To: Ron Moody, Customer Service Manager, Area HQ
Date: Today
Subject: The theft of metal

_____

_____

_____

_____

_____

_____

_____

_____

_____

_____

_____

_____

_____

_____

_____

_____

_____

_____

_____

_____

_____

_____

_____

_____

_____

_____

_____

_____

_____

_____

WRITTEN EXERCISE 10

Right-wing demonstration

Candidate information

In this exercise there are six pages of information.

1. Memorandum from Ron Moody, Customer Service Manager, Area HQ.
2. Article from the *Eastshire Times*.
3. Letter from Muhtarem Mustafa.
4. Letter from Sandra MacLean, Shop Watch.
5. E-mail from Sgt Mark Thompson.
6. Eastshire Shopping Centre Equal Opportunities Statement.

You are to provide a written response (a blank form is provided on which to place your answer).

Candidate information 10.1

Memorandum

To: Customer Service Officer, Eastshire Branch
From: Customer Service Manager, Area HQ
Date: Yesterday
Subject: Right-wing demonstration

Dear Colleague,

Please find attached documents related to the proposed demonstration and march by the right-wing organisation, the Megiddo Army Front (MAF). The police have asked if we have any preferences regarding the route of the march. I am sorry I can't assist you any further, but I am off on a fact-finding trip to the Himalayas.

Please read and compare the various sources and write a report outlining any issues and potential solutions you feel are appropriate.

Ron Moody

Ron Moody

Customer Service Manager, Area HQ

Candidate information 10.2

Eastshire Times

Right-wing march

By Holly Bright

Residents of Eastshire were shocked to hear of a proposed demonstration and march to be held by the Megiddo Army Front (MAF). Ross Gibbings of the Eastshire police said: 'I can confirm that an application has been made by Mr Smith to march from the railway station, along the High Street and past the front row of the Eastshire Shopping Centre, to finish at the memorial statue next to the market square. We will be liaising with various interested parties and members of the community to identify whether or not the proposed route is appropriate. I would urge the members of public to contact us if they feel in any way concerned about this demonstration. At this stage it is too early to give an estimate of the numbers involved.'

The Eastshire Times is led to understand that Mr Smith has given notice in writing to the police and in doing so has abided by the law under the Public Order Act 1986. Needless to say, many people are not at all happy about the proposed march. Sachvinder Kaur Mahal, the owner of the Sari Shop, said: 'We have worked peacefully here for years, and I find it very upsetting that these people should want to demonstrate in Eastshire.' Dan Lewis from the Spear in Hand public house said: 'I think, being a gay pub, we may close just for that day. No one will want to be here with the right-wing bully boys around anyway. What's the point in making life difficult for yourself?'

A local shopper, who just wanted to be named as George, said: 'I've lived here for years and there has never been anything like this that I can think of. Who is this Smith bloke anyway? You can tell him that he and his kind are not wanted here and we don't want him stirring up any trouble!' These feelings were shared by Mark Pearce, owner of the popular restaurant chain Pie and Mash, who added: 'The thing we pride ourselves on in Eastshire is the ability to get along with each other no matter where people are from. People don't want this demonstration. Just the thought of it almost puts me off my food.'

Eastshire appears not to be at all happy about the demonstration. We put this to Mr Smith, who countered: 'We are doing nothing wrong. This is still a free country, just.'

Candidate information 10.3

Letter from Muhtarem Mustafa

Dear Mr Moody,

I have heard about a proposed demonstration and march by the Megiddo Army Front. The Eastshire Times newspaper said that it would be going past the front row of the shopping centre. As you know, my Halal shop is one of those in the front row.

My family and I live above the shop and we are very worried about what may happen to us. I think I will not be open when they demonstrate. What can you do to help us please?

Yours sincerely,

Muhtarem Mustafa

Muhtarem Mustafa

Candidate information 10.4

Letter from Sandra MacLean, Shop Watch

Dear Mr Moody,

I am contacting you as a representative of the Shop Watch scheme. The scheme has a problem with the proposed demonstration and march by the Megiddo Army Front. In all, we have identified 15 shops and premises that are run by people from a visible ethnic minority background. We are very concerned that the demonstration may become violent and, although the only shop that is directly along the route of the procession is the Halal shop, we feel very concerned for the safety and well-being of the other people and premises. Obviously, we will be writing to the police to try and prevent the demonstration. However, what can you do to guarantee the safety of our community?

Yours sincerely,

Sandra MacLean

Sandra MacLean

Shop Watch

Candidate information 10.5

E-mail from Sgt Mark Thompson

From: markthompson@eastshirepolice.uk
To: ronaldtarquinmoody@eastshirecentre.ds.uk
Date: Yesterday
Subject: Proposed right-wing demonstration and march

Dear Mr Moody,

I am the Police Sergeant for the Eastshire Safer Neighbourhood team. Regarding the MAF demo, we can't stop it because it is watertight and legal. The best we can do is damage limitation. We have one of two options.

- We can restrict the route. I notice that the current application is for there to be a procession along the High Street and past the front row of shops in your centre. We can redirect this to West Street via Moon Street and then into the marketplace if you wish.

- We can permit the march to continue on its original course and flood the area outside the premises with police.

Obviously, there will be a large police presence, but we find prevention to be better than cure in these circumstances.

Mark Thompson

Sergeant, Eastshire Police

Candidate information 10.6

Eastshire Shopping Centre Equal Opportunities Statement

Policy: 23689
Date: 17 May 2002
Topic: Equal opportunities

The Eastshire Shopping Centre seeks to employ a workforce that reflects the diversity of background and culture within which we operate and to provide a working environment free from any form of harassment, intimidation, victimisation or unjustifiable discrimination.

We shall treat individuals openly and fairly and with dignity and respect. We shall value their contribution towards providing a quality service to the people of Eastshire.

All members of the Eastshire Shopping Centre will demonstrate their commitment to these principles and will challenge behaviour that is unacceptable, in particular on the grounds of nationality, gender, race, colour, ethnic or national origin, disability, sexual orientation or marital status.

We shall ensure that our policies and procedures reflect these principles. This applies to all establishments within the Eastshire Shopping Centre.

WRITTEN EXERCISE 10

Report

From: Candidate, Customer Service
To: Ron Moody, Customer Service Manager, Area HQ
Date: Today
Subject: Right-wing demonstration

Part 3
Specimen responses

This final part of the book offers a suggested response for each of the written exercise tasks. Here, you can compare your responses to those shown below. Don't worry if you have responded differently, as there are many possible ways to answer each of the tasks.

The mnemonic ICED is included within the examples to provide structure. Of course, you may have your own structure or mnemonic, and it is good practice to indicate each part in your own work. By doing this, you will know where you are in your writing and this will assist you in identifying what you are doing at any time, for example introducing the problem or offering effective interventions, etc.

WRITTEN EXERCISE 1

Specimen response sheet

Report

From: Candidate, Customer Service
To: Ron Moody, Customer Service Manager, Area HQ
Date: Today
Subject: Parking in Central Parade

(Briefly **introduce** the report)

This report considers the proposal for reducing the amount of time people are permitted to park their vehicles in the Central Parade area. The problem appears to be that many of the people using the parking facilities are elderly and it is suggested that the time available is insufficient to support their needs. This report considers the issues and possible solutions.

(Explain the **circumstances**)

Central Parade offers parking for people for up to two hours at a time. Research indicates that the majority of users, just under 80 per cent, are retired persons, the elderly or disabled members of the community. It is proposed by the council that the time available for parking is reduced to 20 minutes. This may present difficulties for many of the people identified in the research. For example, a letter from Mr Chipperfield suggests that 20 minutes would be insufficient time for him to complete his shopping. This argument is supported by a recent newspaper article from the Eastshire Times, which suggests that many of the local businesses may be influenced adversely, for example Bonnie Hall, a hairdresser, who observes that her customers typically require over an hour for their hair to be styled.

To compound this issue, Eastshire Lib Dem Cllr Sunil Patel draws attention to the fact that some businesses within the centre are struggling already. He also highlights the issue of people parking their vehicles in residential areas.

However, a spokesman for the Eastshire Borough Council suggests that the proposed parking restrictions would allow customers to make only brief stops, which would be good for business, as the turnover of potential customers would increase.

(Describe the various **effective interventions** available)

We have a number of possible effective interventions open to us.

1. Support the council's parking proposal.

2. Resist the proposed changes.

3. Identify a suitable compromise.

(State the details of any proposed **decision** and conclude with a proposal)

I feel that option 1 is inappropriate because the research clearly indicates that, due to the requirements of those parking in Central Parade, the time made available for customers to park their vehicles should be increased. It is a possibility that the council is motivated by the increased revenue as a result of the increase in customers.

Pursuing option 2 would damage our relationship with the borough council, but the needs of the local community come first.

Option 3 suggests that we agree to the reduction in the time available to our customers to some degree, but this, I would argue, is not an option as the research suggests that more time is required for our customers, not less.

I believe that the evidence available supports a stand against any reduction in the amount of time our customers are permitted to park their vehicles. If anything, the time should be increased to suit the needs of people who use the Eastshire Shopping Centre. I propose that we resist any changes to the amount of time people are permitted to park and that a letter is sent to the council requesting that the time allowed be increased to three hours.

WRITTEN EXERCISE 2

Specimen response sheet

Report

From: Candidate, Customer Service
To: Ron Moody, Customer Service Manager, Area HQ
Date: Today
Subject: The removal of the Hayway Playground

(Briefly **introduce** the report)

This report considers the proposal for removing the Hayway Playground and childminding facilities. The issue appears to be that many people rely on the facilities offered at the playground to look after their children as they use the Eastshire Shopping Centre. This report considers the issues and possible solutions.

(Explain the **circumstances**)

The Hayway Playground benefits from being supervised by dedicated staff whose responsibilities include looking after children while their parents do their shopping. The ages of the children range from 3 to 12 years. On any day the playground is attended by 60 to 100 children, at various times. This represents a significant contribution to the safety of the children within the Eastshire Shopping Centre, and they further benefit from the physical activities offered at the playground.

A recent report in the Eastshire Times identified that David Ward, the Cultural and Community Development Manager, has looked into the possibility of relocating the play areas, but as yet has been unable to find a suitable alternative site. The reason for the removal of these facilities is the introduction of flood alleviation works in association with the Eastshire Valley Scheme. It appears that it is not that the playground itself will be subject to flooding, but that the council wish to position a flood basin at that location to collect excess rainwater in the event of a flood. Although the council has proposed that the playground can return once the work has been completed, it has been suggested by the Eastshire Times that this is not the case.

The effect of removing these facilities is highlighted in a letter sent to Mr Moody by Sam Denton, in which he or she explains the benefit of access to the shopping centre by use of the wooden bridge near the playground. Sam Denton explains that, if the bridge was to be removed, it would not be worthwhile attending the shopping centre because of the distance he or she would have to travel. Further benefits include the childminding facilities, as Sam has five children who are looked after at the playground while Sam does the shopping.

(Describe the various **effective interventions** available)

We have a number of possible effective interventions open to us.

1. Support the council's proposal and close the playground.

2. Resist the proposed changes.

3. Identify a suitable compromise.

4. Consider what other resources are available within the centre.

(State the details of any proposed **decision** and conclude with a proposal)

Option 1 is inappropriate because the research clearly indicates that many children benefit from using the playground. Based on the information to hand, it appears unlikely that the location is subject to flooding, just that it is proposed to build a flood basin in that location. Perhaps the basin can be relocated. However, we are not in a position to guarantee that the children will not be in danger from the effect of flooding and, therefore, must opt for a safer option.

Pursuing option 2 would be inappropriate if it meant that the children would be placed in any danger. At present, we just don't know, so further research would be appropriate.

Option 3 might ensure that, if the playground is relocated, a suitable location is found, and this links with option 4, where we can identify what is available within the centre.

Based on the information provided, it seems appropriate to adopt an approach in which we attempt to accommodate both the needs of the borough council and the patrons of the playground. This can be achieved by pre-empting the need to move the playground before another location has been identified as being suitable. I propose we find a suitable location, perhaps with the assistance of the Eastshire Times and various local businesses.

WRITTEN EXERCISE 3

Specimen response sheet

Report

From: Candidate, Customer Service
To: Ron Moody, Customer Service Manager, Area HQ
Date: Today
Subject: The parking situation at the Muslim Education Centre

(Briefly **introduce** the report)

This report considers the problem experienced by many parking their vehicles in the proximity of the Eastshire Muslim Education Centre. This report considers the issues and possible solutions.

(Explain the **circumstances**)

A recent Eastshire Times article commented upon two separate issues centred on the Eastshire Muslim Education Centre. The first is that of a proposed morgue to be included within the centre. This is not an issue that is considered appropriate for our attention and is being dealt with by the borough council. It appears that the planning application is attracting attention due to the frustration of many who experience difficulty parking their vehicles during prayer times. The centre does benefit from a car park, which provides 50 spaces; however, a letter from Roger McMillan suggests that there can be between 190 and 350 people arriving for prayer. He adds that people using the Eastshire Shopping Centre car park for the purpose of shopping are unable to find a parking space due to the large numbers of people parking their cars and attending the Muslim centre.

The number of vehicles being used for this purpose is not clear. What is clear is that there are too few parking spaces available and, as a consequence, the article in the newspaper appears to identify the beginnings of racial tension between the people using the Muslim centre and others wishing to park locally.

A report from the Eastshire Shopping Centre Research Unit supports Roger McMillan's observations. It further identifies that the prayer time changes each day in accordance with the daylight hours.

However, the report in the Eastshire Times notes that Michael Rowan, from the nearby Tennis and Bowls Club, has offered 250 parking spaces for those wishing to pray at the mosque. It appears that the club is no more than five minutes' walking distance from the mosque.

(Describe the various **effective interventions** available)

We have a number of possible effective interventions open to us. These include:

1. allocating a number of spaces for those who wish to pray at certain times;

2. limiting the amount of time shoppers can park their vehicles in the centre car park;

3. building more car parking spaces for the mosque and the shopping centre;

4. employing the use of the Tennis and Bowls Club's car park.

(State the details of any proposed **decision** and conclude with a proposal)

Option 1 is unworkable due to the variations in the times that people at the mosque pray.

Option 2 is inappropriate because it is highly likely to upset the shoppers and is, therefore, unlikely to contribute to racial cohesion.

Option 3 is expensive and, although workable, will not solve the problem in the short term.

Option 4 appears to be a suitable, perhaps short-term, answer to the problem.

I believe that the evidence available supports the need to accept the kind offer of using the Tennis and Bowls Club's car park. I propose that a meeting be held and Mr Osborn, Mr Rashid, Roger McMillan and Michael Rowan be invited to discuss a viable arrangement that is fair to all concerned.

WRITTEN EXERCISE 4

Specimen response sheet

Report

From: Candidate, Customer Service
To: Ron Moody, Customer Service Manager, Area HQ
Date: Today
Subject: Expanding the drink limit zone

(Briefly **introduce** the report)

This report considers the issue faced by the owners of Roscarlos – a small supermarket-type shop in the Eastshire Shopping Centre. They have expressed concern in relation to the effect that the 'cumulative impact zone' legislation may have on their business. This report considers the issues and possible solutions.

(Explain the **circumstances**)

According to the Eastshire Times, the Eastshire Borough Council's executive has agreed that officers can start consultation with authorities on expanding the current 'cumulative impact zone' as part of the alcohol saturation policy. This policy aims to restrict the number of licensed premises in an area where crime, disorder and nuisance from the premises are a problem. The council officers have indicated that the effect of the policy will be to create a presumption that an application for a premises licence or club premises certificate will be refused unless the applicant can demonstrate that this will not add to the area's issues or impact on one or more of their objectives. There are four licensing objectives:

1. prevention of crime and disorder;

2. prevention of public nuisance;

3. promotion to public safety;

4. protection of children from harm.

Rosano Romualdez and Carlos Fracisco, the owners of Roscarlos, have written to us expressing concern that their business would be adversely affected by this legislation. Their premises open at 9 a.m. and close at 6 p.m., Monday to Saturday. They sell goods that are typical of a small supermarket. The licence they have applied for would enable them to sell alcohol only to be consumed off the premises.

(Describe the various **effective interventions** available)

Comparing their particular situation to the legislation, they do not appear to breach any of the four listed objectives. Closing at 6 p.m. means that they will not contribute to any crime and disorder issues; likewise, it is unlikely that their shop will contribute to any public nuisance or lack of public safety. This legislation is aimed at the kind of typical disturbances experienced at closing time on Friday and Saturday nights. Rosano and Carlos have nothing to fear, as the legislation is not aimed at their type of business.

We have a number of possible options. These include:

1. a letter being sent to the owners of Roscarlos explaining the situation;

2. letters being sent to the other small businesses explaining the situation.

(State the details of any proposed **decision** and conclude with a proposal)

Options 1 and 2 do not go far enough in allaying the fears of the owners of Roscarlos or those of other businesses in the centre.

I propose that I attend in person and speak to the owners of the shop to explain in detail the implications of the legislation and how it will not affect them adversely. Further, a meeting of all the businesses in the Eastshire Shopping Centre must be called, in order to explain the finer details of the Licensing Act 2003 and, in particular, the cumulative impact zone and its effect on them.

WRITTEN EXERCISE 5

Specimen response sheet

Report

From: Candidate, Customer Service
To: Ron Moody, Customer Service Manager, Area HQ
Date: Today
Subject: The closure of 200 spaces at the Eastshire Shopping Centre car park

(Briefly **introduce** the report)

This report considers the issue of the reduced parking available within the Eastshire Shopping Centre car park and the effect it is likely to have on those wishing to use the car park and on local businesses.

(Explain the **circumstances**)

According to the Eastshire Times, parts of the Eastshire Shopping Centre (ESC) car park are in need of resurfacing. It is anticipated that work will begin in two months' time when the first and second floors of the ESC multi-storey car park are to be resurfaced. Only the top floor of three will remain serviceable. This will mean that parking will be reduced from 300 spaces to only 120 spaces. The work will take five days to complete. To complicate this issue, there are 20 people from the Eastshire Leisure Centre who pay £55 for gold membership, which includes a parking space. Some local businesses are also unhappy about the proposals.

The parking that will remain includes 80 pay and display spaces, 20 spaces reserved for those having gold membership of the leisure centre, 10 spaces for disabled people and 10 spaces for parents/guardians accompanied by children.

(Describe the various **effective interventions** available)

There are several options available to us, but the two most appropriate are as follows.

1. Using the Railway Station car park. Here, 350 hundred spaces are available, of which only 200 are used by travellers. This is about five minutes away from the ESC on foot. The cost for parking here is £2.50 per day, compared to the ESC parking at £1 per hour. Within this option the 20 spaces reserved for those having gold membership of the leisure centre, 10 spaces for disabled people and 10 spaces for parents/guardians accompanied by children remain available to those users.

2. The parking at the High Street car park (80 metered spaces, £1 per hour) and East Hill Road car park (unrestricted parking for 60 cars) is made available to those wishing to use the shopping centre. Both are about 15–20 minutes' walk from the shopping centre; however, to compensate for this we introduce a park and ride system at the expense of the centre. Within this option the 20 spaces reserved for those having gold membership

of the leisure centre, 10 spaces for disabled people and 10 spaces for parents/guardians accompanied by children remain available to those users.

(State the details of any proposed **decision** and conclude with a proposal)

Option 1 will be a cheap and convenient alternative, but there is a potential for conflict to arise between those wishing to travel and those wishing to shop.

Option 2 represents a significant cost to the organisation and may be less popular with the shoppers.

I propose that option 1 is adopted, as this will not only provide a convenient alternative parking site, but it will mean that the Eastshire Shopping Centre will not be burdened with the cost of the park and ride facility. The situation can be closely monitored and changed as necessary. Further, an explanation of this proposal and the location of all alternative parking should be communicated to Eastshire residents as necessary.

WRITTEN EXERCISE 6

Specimen response sheet

Report

From: Candidate, Customer Service
To: Ron Moody, Customer Service Manager, Area HQ
Date: Today
Subject: Season ticket protest

(Briefly **introduce** the report)

This report considers four issues associated with reduced parking being available within the Eastshire Shopping Centre (ESC) car park.

1. The effect that the alternative parking proposals are having on people wishing to use the trains.

2. The lack of parking spaces within the ESC car park.

3. A potential increase in crime in relation to vehicles parked in the Eastshire High Street and East Hill Road car parks.

4. An act of criminal damage to a vehicle parked in the East Hill Road car park.

(Explain the **circumstances**)

Recently, a report was submitted outlining the proposals for alternative parking arrangements during the resurfacing work on floors 1 and 2 of the ESC car park. Since that time it has emerged that cracks have been found in the floors, due to the weight of some of the larger vehicles using the car park. As a result, further work is anticipated to repair these cracks that will take approximately two months.

The original report had not anticipated the repairs taking so long and proposed what was a short-term option that could be reviewed as necessary. It appears to be time to review our arrangements.

Further, Misha Yakovleva has complained about the lack of available parking at the Railway Station car park and an act of criminal damage to his or her car at the alternative East Hill Road car park.

(Describe the various **effective interventions** available)

In light of the present situation, there appears to be only one option that is available to us. The most effective intervention is to increase the available parking by making more use of the High Street car park, which benefits from 80 metered spaces at £1 per hour, and the East Hill Road car park, which has unrestricted parking for 60 cars.

Both are about 15–20 minutes' walk from the shopping centre; however, to compensate for this we can introduce a park and ride scheme at the expense of the centre. It is further anticipated that increasing the amount of activity in that area, that is by people waiting for the bus, will act as a deterrent for would-be criminals, as highlighted by Sgt Thompson.

In relation to the incidence of criminal damage at East Hill Road, it is appropriate to ask for an increased police presence in that area and to investigate the use of CCTV. Further, perhaps we could employ the use of some of our own security guards to patrol the area.

(State the details of any proposed **decision** and conclude with a proposal)

I propose that the above interventions be adopted and that Sgt Thompson be informed of the proposals in a meeting I will have with him. I will propose that the security guards' patrols are extended to include the High Street and East Hill Road car parks. Further, I will propose that the Eastshire Times be contacted by me and informed of the positive action we intend to take.

WRITTEN EXERCISE 7

Specimen response sheet

Report

From: Candidate, Customer Service
To: Ron Moody, Customer Service Manager, Area HQ
Date: Today
Subject: The increase in road traffic collisions

(Briefly **introduce** the report)

This report considers the increase in accidents involving pedestrians crossing Railway Approach to enter the Eastshire Shopping Centre. Apparently the zebra crossing has been removed and people are finding it difficult to cross the road safely.

(Explain the **circumstances**)

Recently a number of reports have been submitted in relation to the knock-on effects of the resurfacing work on floors 1 and 2 of the Eastshire Shopping Centre car park. These reports included proposals to use alternative parking facilities to cope with the demand for parking while the Eastshire car park is repaired. An unforeseen consequence of this has been an increase in the number of pedestrians being hit by vehicles as they attempt to cross Railway Approach.

A recent report in the Eastshire Times quoted the local police as observing that the problem is that the car park is designed for people using the railway station, so there is nothing to assist people in crossing the road. Apparently, there was an old style zebra crossing used by people on that stretch of the road, but the council did not replace it the last time the road was resurfaced. As a result, pedestrians are being put in a position of danger as they attempt to cross the road. The reason for there being no crossing facilities, the council said in that article, is that, at the time, research was undertaken to identify if it was economically feasible to replace the crossing with a more up-to-date pedestrian crossing. Their research indicated that very few pedestrians crossed the road at that point. It appeared that nearly 99.9 per cent of those using the station used bicycles, drove or were driven to get there. As a result, they decided that there was no need to replace any form of pedestrian crossing at that point.

This situation has generated criticism from some of the local shoppers, who have expressed annoyance that people have been directed to park their cars in the car park but not be provided with a safe means of crossing the road. The speed limit in front of the railway station is 40 miles per hour. The figures provided indicate a sharp increase in road accidents in December to February. March is included, but only the first two weeks are available at present; however, this month indicated an increase in accidents.

Road Watch, a local government organisation set up to identify significant issues in relation to the use of our roads, has contacted the Eastshire Shopping Centre as it has identified a distinct increase in road casualties. Its representative suggests that we must act as soon as possible as it is obvious that this situation is intolerable. Road Watch suggests that it can offer advice in relation to our options and has contacted Sgt Mark Thompson in relation to this matter. Apparently he is unable to supply any extra patrolling officers due to sickness and annual leave.

(Describe the various **effective interventions** available)

There are several effective interventions available to us.

1. Contact the local authority and introduce a temporary road crossing system with automatic traffic lights.
2. Equip our security guards with high-visibility clothing and assist people in crossing the road.
3. Request a reduction in the speed limit from 40 mph to 20 mph in the affected section of Station Approach.
4. Build a bridge over the road to prevent further accidents.
5. Implement the park and ride system to include the Railway Station car park.

(State the details of any proposed **decision** and conclude with a proposal)

I propose a combination of the above options; these are included in order of perceived availability.

- Our security guards to be appropriately equipped and utilised as crossing patrol operatives (2).
- The local authority to be contacted with a view to supplying temporary crossing lights at the earliest opportunity (1).
- The park and ride to be implemented as from now (5).
- A request to be made to the relevant authority for the speed limit to be reduced with immediate effect (3).
- A pedestrian bridge to be built over the road (4).

I will take personal responsibility to see that optionss 2, 1, and 5 are implemented with immediate effect. We have a duty of care to our customers.

WRITTEN EXERCISE 8

Specimen response sheet

Report

From: Candidate, Customer Service
To: Ron Moody, Customer Service Manager, Area HQ
Date: Today
Subject: The wearing of hoodies

(Briefly **introduce** the report)

This report considers the issue of the council's recent proposal to ban people from wearing hoodies within the Eastshire Shopping Centre. The subject will be considered from the various perspectives and recommendations made.

(Explain the **circumstances**)

The circumstances are that, in a recent report in the Eastshire Times, Holly Bright reported that, under new regulations to be introduced next month, any person found wearing a hoodie will be asked to leave the premises. The article contains a response from a parent saying that a hoodie is what her children want to wear, and one businessman alludes to the fact that not all people who wear hoodies are criminals. However, countering this assertion is a quote from a local pensioner who was mugged by a person wearing a hoodie. Needless to say, he is in agreement that the wearing of them should be banned. He does, though, hit on an important issue: that they appear to be worn by people who wish to hide their identity from CCTV.

Sgt Thompson, of the Safer Neighbourhood team, also features in the report and highlights the issue of reasonableness, suggesting that 'What we must ask ourselves is this – is it a reasonable thing to ask people not to wear hoodies because it makes some people feel uneasy? Yes, the kids have rights, but so does everyone else. If hoodies were not linked to crime, there would be no problem, but the sad fact is, they are.'

The problem is compounded by a situation highlighted by Keith Giannoni, manager of the Olympic Body gym. In a letter, he stated that he recently provided his 20 gold members with top of the range leisure wear as a thank you for their loyalty to the gym. This included a hooded sweat top with his logo emblazoned on the chest. Many of those members arrive and leave the gym in their tops. He threatens that, if the council's recommendation is pursued, he will consider finding an alternative venue for his gym, as the ban will include his members.

During our research, we contacted Chrissie Coles, a renowned expert in the study of teenage social behaviour who works as an adviser to the government. In her report, she identified the issues faced by teenagers in respect to their opinions and feelings in a local blog. In essence, the report appears to highlight a similar opinion to that held by Sgt Thompson and

Mr Reid, a local retailer, that those engaged in crime often wear hoodies, but not all those wearing hoodies are involved in crime.

(Describe the various **effective interventions** available)

There are two main positions held in this case: that of the council, who wish to ban the wearing of hoodies altogether; and that of those (mainly teenagers) who prefer to wear this item of clothing.

We have three options:

1. ban hoodies;

2 permit hoodies;

3. permit hoodies on the understanding that the hoods are to be kept down when in and around the shopping centre.

(State the details of any proposed **decision** and conclude with a proposal)

Option 1 will have the effect of disadvantaging the many honest young people who attend the centre. Further, it will antagonise Mr Giannoni, who has invested in hoodies for his gold members. Option 2 will send a message to the council and police alike that we are not willing to help or are not interested in combating crime. This is not the case. Option 3 is an ideal compromise because it will not infringe on people's liberties and will ensure that they are able to be identified.

I propose that we adopt option 3 and ensure that the rules are enforced rigorously and that any person wearing a hood covering their face will be removed from the centre immediately. I will contact Holly Bright, the police and the local authority explaining what we are doing and the reasons for this.

WRITTEN EXERCISE 9

Specimen response sheet

Report

From: Candidate, Customer Service
To: Ron Moody, Customer Service Manager, Area HQ
Date: Today
Subject: The theft of metal

(Briefly **introduce** the report)

This report considers the growing crime of the theft of metal. It appears that, recently, the price of metal has increased so that the return on scrap metal is relatively high. Apparently this is funding some people's drug addiction.

(Explain the **circumstances**)

According to a recent article in the Eastshire Times, scrap metal thieves are stealing metal from a wide variety of sources, such as church and school roofs and drain-hole covers in the Eastshire area. The thefts have been made attractive to the thieves due to the soaring price of metals around the world. The article suggests that much of the stolen metal and copper cabling is sold to illegal dealers who sell it off to be shipped abroad. The Safer Eastshire Partnership, which includes Eastshire Borough Council and the Eastshire police, is asking the public to help stem the theft by supplying information on suspicious behaviour that could lead to arrests. These activities include dismantling motor vehicles and storing large quantities of industrial cabling on property.

According to Inspector Dino Gomez, last month, two men who were trying to steal hundreds of feet of electricity cable awaiting installation by contractors were sentenced at Eastshire Crown Court. The partnership points out that the Scrap Metal Dealers' Act demands that any person or business dealing in scrap metal is registered with the council and that all records must be kept for examination on demand.

Lindsey Thornberg, from the Shop Watch scheme, contacted us stating that they have a problem that only became apparent after they realised that what they thought were one-offs were in fact a pattern of behaviour; people are stealing metal. All Hallows Church, now known as the Eastshire Muslim Education Centre, had the lead and copper from its roof stolen and, last week, the Eastshire Primary School had its copper roof stolen. The cost of repairing the two roofs is estimated to be in excess of £80,000. Further, the Buddha statue was also taken from outside the temple; this is irreplaceable.

Small businesses are suffering from similar thefts; for example, the cover for the drains has been taken and the metal stands used for the market have completely disappeared. Incredibly someone had tried to steal the copper power lines from the electricity substation while they were live. Dominic Gannon from Drugs Watch notes a clear link between the theft of metal and feeding drug habits. He suggests that the key to prevention is to make the community more aware of what is happening, make them inquisitive and provide them with someone who can assist them in the event of any suspicious behaviour.

(Describe the various **effective interventions** available)

There are several effective interventions available, but their implementation may be reliant upon the availability of sufficient funding.

1. Increased use of CCTV.

2. Increased patrols by our security guards.

3. Increased patrols by the police.

4. A volunteer to monitor the phones and collate relevant information.

5. To liaise more closely with the police for the purposes of intelligence.

6. To increase the awareness of the public.

(State the details of any proposed **decision** and conclude with a proposal)

No particular option is more or less important than any other. I propose that it is the combination of all of the above options that will contribute to a reduction in the theft of metal. To this end, I will volunteer to establish a steering group to achieve these goals.

WRITTEN EXERCISE 10

Specimen response sheet

Report

From: Candidate, Customer Service
To: Ron Moody, Customer Service Manager, Area HQ
Date: Today
Subject: Right-wing demonstration

(Briefly **introduce** the report)

This report considers the pros and cons of a proposed demonstration and march by the Megiddo Army Front (MAF), an extreme right-wing group, and is written in response to a request from the Eastshire police.

(Explain the **circumstances**)

According to Ross Gibbings of the Eastshire police, an application has been made by Mr Smith from the MAF to march from the railway station, along the High Street and past the front row of the Eastshire Shopping Centre, to finish at the memorial statue next to the market square. By making this application Mr Smith has abided by the law under the Public Order Act 1986. The effect of this, according to the Eastshire Times, has been to cause concern among some ethnic minority groups who live and work in Eastshire. The owners of a local gay pub are considering closing for the day to prevent any trouble.

Muhtarem Mustafa, a local shop owner, has written to us describing his worries that the demonstration will pass in front of his shop. He has asked what we can do to help him.

A representative from the Shop Watch scheme has also written to us in relation to the proposed demonstration by the MAF. In all the scheme has identified 15 shops and premises that are run by people from a visible ethnic minority background. Shop Watch is very worried that the demonstration may become violent and, although the only such shop that is directly along the route of the procession is the Halal shop, owned by Mr Mustafa, it feels very concerned for the safety and well-being of the other people and premises. It, too, asks what we can do to guarantee the safety of our community.

We are guided by our own Equal Opportunities Statement, which offers principles and guidance when dealing with others. It states that we will 'provide a working environment free from any form of harassment, intimidation, victimisation or unjustifiable discrimination', and that we will 'challenge behaviour that is unacceptable, in particular on the grounds of nationality, gender, race, colour, ethnic or national origin, disability, sexual orientation or marital status'.

Our responsibilities extend not only to each other but to our customers. Therefore, we expect others to conform to these principles and this includes the MAF.

(Describe the various **effective interventions** available)

I have sought the advice of Sgt Mark Thompson of the Eastshire police, who suggests that the demonstration cannot be stopped because Mr Smith has conformed to the law. He offers two options.

1. We can restrict the route. I notice that the current application is for there to be a procession along the High Street and past the front row of shops in your centre. We can redirect this to West Street via Moon Street and then into the marketplace if you wish.

2. We can permit the march to continue on its original course and flood the area outside the premises with police.

Sgt Thompson adds that we can rely on a large police presence.

(State the details of any proposed **decision** and conclude with a proposal)

I propose that option 1 be adopted, and that the demonstration is redirected away from the Halal shop. Police will need to be supported by our security guards and will have radios shared between them to maximise communication.

Further, all ethnic minority premises should remain open if possible and a dedicated line of communication should be established via a mobile phone number.

All security guard leave will be cancelled and consideration will be given to the ethnic origin of the security guards and the duties they perform.

Appendix A

Answers to Part 1 tasks

Task 1 (page 6)

Step 3, because being unconsciously competent at Step 4 means that you are doing it correctly but no longer have to identify why. Step 3 enables you to question what you have done and you are able to take care to ensure that your work is correct.

Task 2 (page 13)

The police service of the twenty-first centery (century) relys (relies) on the willingness of the communitties (communities) too (to) be policed.

Task 3 (page 15)

1. She found the police officers were very helpful.
2. As she searched the house, she noticed the room was full of toys for babies.
3. 'I am getting fed up with all these taxes,' the inspector complained.
4. Of all the capital cities, London is my favourite.
5. As you look over the rooftops towards Hampton Court, you can see hundreds of chimneys.
6. The sun's rays burst through the clouds like fingers pointing at the ground.
7. She was a petite women (woman).
8. He said that all of his tooths (teeth) hurt.
9. The aircrafts (aircraft) were screaming across the sky.
10. He was using his binocular (binoculars) to see the deers (deer).

Task 4 (page 16)

1. It's as I said; you know I allways (always) tell the truth, well allmost (almost). I may have had a gun in my hand standing outside the bank, officor (officer). But I had no idea there was an armed robbery taking place inside the bank; there was quite a fus (fuss). In fact, I found the gun on the floor and was going to hand it to you. Luckily you came around the corner, found me and siezed (seized) the gun.

2. I was told that, if I wanted to recieve (receive) less spam, I would have to place a cross in the box.

3. You don't deceive me; you have hidden the money by carefully taping each note to the cieling (ceiling) and then painting over it.

4. I was hopefull (hopeful) that we would be able to get together, all of us, in the house on the hill, but it was alltogether (altogether) too difficult.

5. The house on the hill, you say? I was allso (also) looking forward to it until I heard that a plane allmost (almost) came through the roof. That's what happens when you leave the landing light on.

6. I don't know what I should do for a living. Allthough (although) I could be a police officer, teacher, tax collecter (collector) or racing driver, I might prefer being a person of leisure.

7. That sounds wonderfull (wonderful)!

Task 5 (page 19)

1. try   –   trying
2. cry   –   crying
3. shoplift   –   shoplifting
4. chop   –   chopping
5. roll   –   rolling
6. escape   –   escaping
7. make   –   making
8. steal   –   stealing
9. lie   –   lying
10. untie   –   untying

Task 6 (page 19)

1. arrogant   –   arrog**ance**
2. resistant –   resist**ance**
3. silent   –   sil**ence**
4. obedient   –   obedi**ence**
5. absent   –   abs**ence**
6. distant   –   dist**ance**
7. intolerant –   intoler**ance**

8. belligerent – belliger**ence**

9. impatient – impati**ence**

10. radiant – radi**ance**

Task 7 (pages 19–20)

1. I carried the water.		Correct
2. I love curry'ed eggs. Alternative spelling: curried		Incorrect
3. Blackberries are wonderful.		Correct
4. Once I supplyed all the police stations with blue lights. Alternative spelling: supplied		Incorrect
5. comfortable		
6. visable	–	visible
7. predictable		
8. understandible	–	understandable
9. flexible		
10. action		
11. reservasion	–	reservation
12. discussion		
13. nation		
14. organisasion	–	organisation
15. divertion	–	diversion

Task 8 (page 21)

As a Police Community Support Officer, I can't weight (wait) two (to) see the fare (fair), as it brings out the best in the local people. I hope it is as good as last year. I was off duty at the time and remember that won (one) ride hurt me so much, it gave me a pane (pain) in my side, witch (which) lasted up too (to) a weak (week). I will sea (see) if the bumper cars are in the same plaice (place); it would be nice to meat (meet) up their (there) again. Although, if eye (I) remember correctly, they maid (made) me feel a little sick. I think the fair is grate (great). What do yew (you) think; am I rite (right) or knot (not)?

Task 9 (pages 20–21)

1. To make a **great** cauliflower cheese you will have to **grate** a lot of cheese.

2. Although the cook **made** the sandwiches, the **maid** served them.

3. It was not uncommon for the **male** members of the cast to receive vast amounts of **mail**.

4. Even **more** birds were found to be nesting on the **moor**.

5. He looked down at his plate where the last **bean** had **been**.

Task 10 (page 24)

1. It's two hot in here.	Incorrect	'too' not 'two'
2. It takes too to tango.	Incorrect	'two' not 'too'
3. Two many crooks spoil the bank job.	Incorrect	'too' not 'two'
4. One, two, three, four.	Correct	
5. They're going to get cold up there.	Correct	
6. Over their, look.	Incorrect	'there' not 'their'
7. By the looks of things, they're busy.	Correct	
8. I was right, they're in the cell.	Correct	
9. You was right, their all out.	Incorrect	'were' not 'was' and 'they're' not 'their'
10. Two was the answer, but that was before one ran off.	Correct	

11. beach – beaches

12. tax – taxes

13. patch – patches

14. bus – buses

15. palace – palaces

16. knife – knives

17. leaf – leaves

18. sheep – sheep

19. half – halves

20. mouse – mice

Appendix B

National Core Competencies

Reproduced in part, with kind permission, from *The Integrated Competency Behavioural Framework Version 9.0 (May 2007)* by Skills for Justice.

1. Respect for race and diversity Considers and shows respect for the opinions, circumstances and feelings of colleagues and members of the public, no matter what their race, religion, position, background, circumstances, status or appearance.

Required level Understands other people's views and takes them into account. Is tactful and diplomatic when dealing with people. Treats them with dignity and respect at all times. Understands and is sensitive to social, cultural and racial differences.

- Sees issues from other people's viewpoints.

- Is polite, tolerant and patient with people inside and outside the organisation, treating them with respect and dignity.

- Respects the needs of everyone involved when sorting out disagreements.

- Shows understanding and sensitivity to people's problems and vulnerabilities.

- Deals with diversity issues and gives positive practical support to staff who may feel vulnerable.

- Listens to and values others' views and opinions.

- Uses language in an appropriate way and is sensitive to the way it may affect people.

- Acknowledges and respects a broad range of social and cultural customs and beliefs and values within the law.

- Understands what offends others and adapts own actions accordingly.

- Respects and maintains confidentiality, where appropriate.

- Delivers difficult messages sensitively.

- Challenges attitudes and behaviour which are abusive, aggressive or discriminatory.

- Takes into account others' personal needs and interests.

- Supports minority groups both inside and outside their organisation.

Negative indicators

- Does not consider other people's feelings.

- Does not encourage people to talk about personal issues.

- Criticises people without considering their feelings and motivation.

- Makes situations worse with inappropriate remarks, language or behaviour.

- Is thoughtless and tactless when dealing with people.

- Is dismissive and impatient with people.

- Does not respect confidentiality.

- Unnecessarily emphasises power and control in situations where this is not appropriate.

- Intimidates others in an aggressive and overpowering way.

- Uses humour inappropriately.

- Shows bias and prejudice when dealing with people.

2. Team working   Develops strong working relationships inside and outside the team to achieve common goals. Breaks down barriers between groups and involves others in discussions and decisions.

Required level   Works effectively as a team member and helps build relationships within it. Actively helps and supports others to achieve team goals.

- Understands own role in a team.

- Actively supports and assists the team to reach their objectives.

- Is approachable and friendly to others.

- Makes time to get to know people.

- Co-operates with and supports others.

- Offers to help other people.

- Asks for and accepts help when needed.

- Develops mutual trust and confidence in others.

- Willingly takes on unpopular or routine tasks.

- Contributes to team objectives no matter what the direct personal benefit may be.

- Acknowledges that there is often a need to be a member of more than one team.

- Takes pride in their team and promotes their team's performance to others.

Negative indicators

- Does not volunteer to help other team members.
- Is only interested in taking part in high-profile and interesting activities.
- Takes credit for success without recognising the contribution of others.
- Works to own agenda rather than contributing to team performance.
- Allows small exclusive groups of people to develop.
- Plays one person off against another.
- Restricts and controls what information is shared.
- Does not let people say what they think.
- Does not offer advice or get advice from others.
- Shows little interest in working jointly with other groups to meet the goals of everyone involved.
- Does not discourage conflict within the organisation.

3. Community and customer focus	Focuses on the customer and provides a high-quality service that is tailored to meet their individual needs. Understands the communities that are served and shows an active commitment to policing that reflects their needs and concerns.
Required level	Provides a high level of service to customers. Maintains contact with customers, works out what they need and responds to them.

- Presents an appropriate image to the public and other organisations.
- Supports strategies that aim to build an organisation that reflects the community it serves.
- Focuses on the customer in all activities.
- Tries to sort out customers' problems as quickly as possible.
- Apologises when they are at fault or have made mistakes.
- Responds quickly to customer requests.
- Makes sure that customers are satisfied with the service they receive.
- Manages customer expectations.
- Keeps customers updated on progress.
- Balances customer needs with organisational needs.

Negative indicators

- Is not customer focused and does not consider individual needs.
- Does not tell customers what is going on.
- Presents an unprofessional image to customers.
- Only sees a situation from their own view, not from the customer's view.
- Shows little interest in the customer – only deals with their immediate problem.
- Does not respond to the needs of the local community.
- Focuses on organisational issues rather than customer needs.
- Does not make the most of opportunities to talk to people in the community.
- Slow to respond to customers' requests.
- Fails to check that the customers' needs have been met.

4. Effective communication	Communicates ideas and information effectively, both verbally and in writing. Uses language and a style of communication that is appropriate to the situation and people being addressed. Makes sure others understand what is going on.
Required level	Communicates all needs, instructions and decisions clearly. Adapts the style of communication to meet the needs of the audience. Checks for understanding.

- Deals with issues directly.
- Clearly communicates needs and instructions.
- Clearly communicates management decisions and policy, and the reasons behind them.
- Communicates face to face wherever possible and if appropriate.
- Speaks with authority and confidence.
- Changes the style of communication to meet the needs of the audience.
- Manages group discussions effectively.
- Summarises information to check people understand it.
- Supports arguments and recommendations effectively in writing.
- Produces well-structured reports and written summaries.

Negative indicators

- Is hesitant, nervous and uncertain when speaking.
- Speaks without first thinking through what to say.

- Uses inappropriate language or jargon.

- Speaks in a rambling way.

- Does not consider the target audience.

- Avoids answering difficult questions.

- Does not give full information without being questioned.

- Writes in an unstructured way.

- Uses poor spelling, punctuation and grammar.

- Assumes others understand what has been said without actually checking.

- Does not listen and interrupts at inappropriate times.

5. Problem solving   Gathers information from a range of sources. Analyses information to identify problems and issues and makes effective decisions.

Required level   Gathers enough relevant information to understand specific issues and events. Uses information to identify problems and draw conclusions. Makes good decisions.

- Identifies where to get information and gets it.

- Gets as much information as is appropriate on all aspects of a problem.

- Separates relevant information from irrelevant information and important information from unimportant information.

- Takes on information quickly and accurately.

- Reviews all the information gathered to understand the situation and to draw logical conclusions.

- Identifies and links causes and effects.

- Identifies what can and cannot be changed.

- Takes a systematic approach to solving problems.

- Remains impartial and avoids jumping to conclusions.

- Refers to procedures and precedents, as necessary, before making decisions.

- Makes good decisions that take account of all relevant factors.

Negative indicators

- Doesn't deal with problems in detail and does not identify underlying issues.

- Does not gather enough information before coming to conclusions.

- Does not consult other people who may have extra information.

- Does not research background.

- Shows no interest in gathering or using intelligence.

- Does not gather evidence.

- Makes assumptions about the facts of a situation.

- Does not recognise problems until they have become significant issues.

- Gets stuck in the detail of complex situations and cannot see the main issues.

- Reacts without considering all the angles.

- Becomes distracted by minor issues.

6. Personal responsibility	Takes personal responsibility for making things happen and achieving results. Displays motivation, commitment, perseverance and conscientiousness. Acts with a high degree of integrity.
Required level	Takes personal responsibility for own actions and for sorting out issues or problems that arise. Is focused on achieving results to required standards and developing skills and knowledge.

- Accepts personal responsibility for own decisions and actions.

- Takes action to resolve problems and fulfil own responsibilities.

- Keeps promises and does not let colleagues down.

- Takes pride in work.

- Is conscientious in completing work on time.

- Follows things through to satisfactory conclusion.

- Displays initiative, taking on tasks without having to be asked.

- Is self-motivated, showing enthusiasm and dedication to their role.

- Focuses on task even if it is routine.

- Improves own professional knowledge and keeps it up to date.

- Is open, honest and genuine, standing up for what is right.

- Makes decisions based upon ethical consideration and organisational integrity.

Negative indicators

- Passes responsibility upwards inappropriately.

- Is not concerned about letting others down.

- Will not deal with issues, just hopes they will go away.

- Blames others rather than admitting to mistakes or looking for help.

- Is unwilling to take on responsibility.

- Puts in the minimum effort that is needed to get by.

- Shows a negative and disruptive attitude.

- Shows little energy and enthusiasm for work.

- Expresses a cynical attitude to the organisation and their job.

- Gives up easily when faced with problems.

- Fails to recognise personal weaknesses and development needs.

- Makes little or no attempt to develop self or keep up to date.

7. Resilience   Shows resilience, even in difficult circumstances. Is prepared to make difficult decisions and has the confidence to see them through.

Required level   Shows reliability and resilience in difficult circumstances. Remains calm and confident and responds logically and decisively in difficult situations.

- Is reliable in a crisis, remains calm and thinks clearly.

- Sorts out conflict and deals with hostility and provocation in a calm and restrained way.

- Responds to challenges rationally, avoiding inappropriate emotion.

- Deals with difficult emotional issues and then moves on.

- Manages conflicting pressures and tensions.

- Maintains professional ethics when confronted with pressure from others.

- Copes with ambiguity and deals with uncertainty and frustration.

- Resists pressure to make quick decisions where consideration is needed.

- Remains focused and in control of situation.

- Makes and carries through decisions, even though they are unpopular, difficult or controversial.

- Stands firmly by a position when it is right to do so.

- Defends their staff from excessive criticisms from outside the team.

Negative indicators

- Gets easily upset, frustrated and annoyed.

- Panics and becomes agitated when problems arise.

- Walks away from confrontation when it would be more appropriate to get involved.

- Needs constant reassurance, support and supervision.

- Uses inappropriate physical force.

- Gets too emotionally involved in situations.

- Reacts inappropriately when faced with rude or abusive people.

- Deals with situations aggressively.

- Complains and whinges about problems rather than dealing with them.

- Gives in inappropriately when under pressure.

- Worries about making mistakes and avoids difficult situations wherever possible.

Index